Collins

KS3
Spanish

Revision Guide

with audio download

Helen Farrar and Sherrie A Spinks

About this Revision & Practice book

When it comes to getting the best results, practice really does make perfect!

Experts have proved that repeatedly testing yourself on a topic is far more effective than re-reading information over and over again. And, to be as effective as possible, you should space out the practice test sessions over time.

This revision guide and workbook is specially designed to support this approach to revision and includes seven different opportunities to test yourself on spelling, punctuation and grammar, spaced out over time.

Revise

These pages provide a recap of everything you need to know for each topic.

You should read through all the information before taking the Quick Test at the end. This will test whether you can recall the key facts.

Practise

These topic-based questions appear shortly after the revision pages for each topic and will test whether you have understood the topic. If you get any of the questions wrong, make sure you read the correct answer carefully.

Review

These topic-based questions appear later in the book, allowing you to revisit the topic and test how well you have remembered the information. If you get any of the questions wrong, make sure you read the correct answer carefully.

Mix it Up

These pages feature a mix of questions for all the different topics, just like you would get in a test. They will make sure you can recall the relevant information to answer a question without being told which topic it relates to.

Test Yourself on the Go

Visit our website at **collins.co.uk/collinsks3revision** and print off a set of flashcards. These pocket-sized cards feature questions and answers so that you can test yourself on all the key facts anytime and anywhere. You will also find lots more information about the advantages of spaced practice and how to plan for it.

Workbook & Audio

This section features even more topic-based and mixed test-style questions, providing two further practice opportunities for each topic to guarantee the best results. Visit our website at **collins.co.uk/collinsks3revision** to download the supporting audio material for essential listening practice.

ebook

To access the ebook visit collins.co.uk/ebooks and follow the step-by-step instructions.

Contents

Family 1

You must be able to:

- Give and ask for personal information such as name, age, birthday and nationality
- Describe your family and give personal details about members of your family, using the he / she / they forms of the verbs
- Use connectives to make longer sentences.

My Name

- **¿Cómo te llamas?**   What's your name?
  Me llamo…   My name is…
- **Mi nombre es…**   My first name is…
- **Mi apellido es…**   My surname is…
- **¿Cómo se escribe tu nombre?**   How do you spell your (first) name?
  Se escribe…   It is spelt…

My Age

- **¿Cuántos años tienes?**   How old are you?
  Tengo trece años.   I am thirteen years old.
  Pronto, voy a cumplir catorce.   Soon, I will be fourteen.
- **¿Cuándo es tu cumpleaños?**   When is your birthday?
  Mi cumpleaños es el siete de julio.   My birthday is on the 7th of July.
- **¿Cuándo naciste?**   When were you born?
  Nací en dos mil nueve.   I was born in 2009.

Where I Live

- **¿Dónde vives?**   Where do you live?
  Vivo en Barcelona en España.   I live in Barcelona in Spain.
- **Soy inglés / inglesa.**   I am English.
  Soy galés / galesa.   I am Welsh.
  Soy español / española.   I am Spanish.

Family Members

- **En mi familia hay…**   In my family there is / are…
  personas.   people.
  En mi familia somos cuatro.   There are four of us in my family.
- **mi madre**   my mum
  mi padre   my dad
  mis padres   my parents
  mi hermana   my sister
  mi hermano   my brother
  mi madrastra   my step-mum

Key Point

Don't forget that when forming questions, you need to use **¿** at the beginning of the question as well as **?** at the end. The same rule applies when using exclamation marks (**¡** and **!**):

¿Cuántos años tienes?

How old are you?

¡Qué guay!

Cool!

mi padrastro	my step-dad
mi hermanastra	my step-sister or half-sister
mi hermanastro	my step-brother or half-brother
mi abuela	my grandmother
mi abuelo	my grandfather
mis abuelos	my grandparents
mi tía	my aunt
mi tío	my uncle
y yo	and me

- **Soy hija única.**   I am an only child (daughter).
  Soy hijo único.   I am an only child (son).
  No tengo hermanos.   I don't have any brothers or sisters / siblings.

- **Soy el hermano mayor.**   I am the oldest brother.
  Soy la hermana menor.   I am the youngest sister.

Information About Others

- **(Ella / Él) Se llama...**   She / He is called...
- **(Ella / Él) Tiene... años.**   She / He is... years old.
- **(Ellas / Ellos) Se llaman...**   They are called...
- **(Ellas / Ellos) Tienen... años.**   They are... years old.
- **Mi hermana se llama Carmen y tiene doce años.**   My sister is called Carmen and she is twelve years old.
  Tengo dos hermanos que se llaman Luis y Jorge y tienen cuatro años.   I have two brothers who are called Luis and Jorge and they are four years old.
  Son gemelos.   They are twins.

Quick Test

1. Say or write what your name is and how old you are in Spanish.
2. Ask someone what their name is and how old they are in Spanish.
3. What is the Spanish for step-sister?
4. Translate the following into English:
   ¡Hola! Me llamo Alicia y pronto voy a cumplir trece años. Mi cumpleaños es el veinticinco de agosto. Vivo en Murcia con mis padres y mis tres hermanos; un hermano y dos hermanas. Mi hermano se llama Diego y tiene diez años. Mis hermanas se llaman María y Luisa y tienen siete años. Son gemelas.

Family 2

You must be able to:

- Give a physical description of yourself and of other people, using adjectives
- Name pets and give a brief description of them, using adjectives
- Use different forms of the verbs **to be** and **to have** (**ser** and **tener**).

Describing Hair and Eyes

tengo I have **él / ella** **tiene** he / she has **ellos / ellas** **tienen** they have	los ojos	eyes	**marrones** **verdes** **azules** **oscuros**	brown green blue dark
	el pelo	hair	**negro** **gris** **castaño** **rubio** **largo** **corto** **(ni) largo** **(ni) corto** **rizado** **ondulado** **liso**	black grey brown blond long short (neither) long (nor) short curly wavy straight

- **Tengo el pelo castaño, liso y largo.**   I have brown, straight, long hair.
  Tengo los ojos azules pero   I have blue eyes but
  mi hermano tiene los ojos verdes.   my brother has green eyes.
- **Mi hermana, que se llama Marisa,**   My sister, who is called Marisa,
  tiene ocho años.   is eight years old.
- **Ella tiene los ojos marrones**   She has brown eyes
  y el pelo rubio, ondulado, y corto.   and blond, wavy, short hair.

Describing Size

		size	masculine	feminine
soy **es**	I am he / she is	small / short	**bajo**	**baja**
		tall	**alto**	**alta**
		slim / thin	**delgado**	**delgada**
		fat	**gordo**	**gorda**

- **Soy muy alto y**   I am very tall and
  bastante delgado, pero   quite slim but
  mi hermana es muy   my sister is very
  baja y bastante gorda.   short and quite fat.

Describing Personality

- Here is a list of useful adjectives. Remember that with most adjectives you need to change the ending according to whether the thing or person you are describing is masculine or feminine. However, some adjectives have the same spelling for masculine and feminine nouns.

	masculine	feminine
shy	**tímido**	**tímida**
friendly	**simpático**	**simpática**
funny	**divertido**	**divertida**
happy	**contento**	**contenta**
cute	**lindo**	**linda**
lazy	**perezoso**	**perezosa**
sad	**triste**	**triste**
annoying	**irritante**	**irritante**
sporty	**deportista**	**deportista**

Soy muy deportista y bastante lindo, pero mi hermana es perezosa y un poco irritante.
I'm very sporty and pretty cute, but my sister is lazy and a little irritating.

Key Point

Use quantifiers to improve your descriptions.

muy	very
bastante	quite
un poco	a little

Describing Pets

¿Tienes animales?	Do you have any pets?
¿Tienes mascotas?	Do you have any pets?
Sí, tengo una mascota.	Yes, I have a pet.
No, no tengo mascota.	No, I don't have a pet.

a dog	**un perro**	a cat	**un gato**
a horse	**un caballo**	a fish	**un pez**
a mouse	**un ratón**	a rabbit	**un conejo**
a bird	**un pájaro**	a tortoise	**una tortuga**
a snake	**una serpiente**	a guinea pig	**un cobayo**

En casa, tengo un perro y unos peces de colores.	At home, I have a dog and some goldfish.
En el establo tengo un caballo.	In the stable I have a horse.

- To describe your pets you can use the same language as when describing people.

Mi conejo se llama Ramón y tiene tres años. Es negro y también es muy lindo. Es mediano.	My rabbit is called Ramón and he is three years old. He is black and he is also very cute. He is medium sized.

Key Vocab

ellos /	they /
ellas tienen	they have
el pelo	hair
él / ella	he / she
es	is
los ojos	eyes
ser	to be
tener	to have
tiene	has

Quick Test

1. Say or write in Spanish: I have long, blond, curly hair and brown eyes.
2. Choose the correct word: **Mi hermana es bajo / baja.**
3. Say you do not have a pet in Spanish.
4. Choose the correct word: **Mi hermano tiene dos gato / gatos.**

House and Home 1

You must be able to:

- Say exactly where you live and the type of home you live in
- Describe your home.

Where I Live

- **¿Dónde vives?** — Where do you live?
  Vivo en... — I live in... (name of town)
  Vivo en Londres. — I live in London.
  Vivo en Inglaterra. — I live in England.
  en Escocia — in Scotland
  en Gales — in Wales
  en Irlanda — in Ireland
  en España — in Spain
  en Gran Bretaña — in Great Britain

My Home

- **Vivo en...** — I live in / on...
  una casa — a house
  una casa adosada — a semi-detached house
  una granja — a farm
  un piso — a flat
  un apartamento — an apartment

Describing Location

- **en una ciudad** — in a city
  en un pueblo — in a town
  en una aldea — in a village
  en el centro del pueblo — in the town centre
  en las afueras — in the suburbs
  en el campo — in the countryside
  al lado del mar — at the seaside
  en las montañas — in the mountains
- **Vivo en una casa grande** — I live in a big house
  en un pueblo pequeño — in a small town
  en el campo. — in the countryside.
- **Vivo cerca de Manchester.** — I live near Manchester.
- **Vivo lejos de Manchester.** — I live far from Manchester.
- **Vivo en Liverpool** — I live in Liverpool
  en el noroeste — in the northwest
  de Inglaterra. — of England.

- **Ella vive en Murcia en España.** She lives in Murcia in Spain.
- **Él vive en el sur de México.** He lives in the south of Mexico.
  el norte the north
  el sur the south
  el este the east
  el oeste the west

Inside my Home

- **En mi casa hay...** In my house there is...
  un salón a living room
  una cocina a kitchen
  un comedor a dining room
  tres habitaciones three bedrooms
  la habitación de mis padres my parents' bedroom
  una sala de estar a living room
  un despacho an office
  un ático an attic
  un sótano a cellar
  un jardín a garden
  un garaje a garage
  un cuarto de baño a bathroom
  una ducha a shower
  un aseo a toilet
  en la planta baja on the ground floor
  en la primera planta on the first floor
  en la segunda planta on the second floor
- **En mi hogar** In my home
  hay... habitaciones. there are... (bed)rooms.
- **En mi casa tenemos** In my house we have
  cuatro habitaciones arriba four bedrooms upstairs
  y tres abajo pero and three downstairs
  no hay **ático.** but there isn't an attic.
- **No hay ni ático ni garaje.** There is neither an attic nor a garage.
- **Comparto mi dormitorio.** I share my bedroom.
- **Tengo mi propio dormitorio.** I have my own bedroom.

Key Point

Rooms in Spanish are either masculine (**el / un**) or feminine (**la / una**). When using adjectives to describe the room you may need to change the endings:

Mi habitación es pequeña y roja.

My bedroom is small and red.

1. Say that you live in a house in a town in the east of England in Spanish.
2. Masculine or feminine? bathroom kitchen garden
3. What is the Spanish word for *far from*?
4. Say that you share a room with your sister in Spanish.

Key Vocab

en mi casa	in my house
hay...	there is...
no hay...	there isn't...
vivo en	I live in / on / at

House and Home 2

You must be able to:

- Name the items of furniture you have at home
- Say where things are, using prepositions
- Say what you do or don't do at home.

Items in the Home

los muebles	furniture
la silla	chair
la mesa	table
el armario	wardrobe
la lámpara	lamp
la televisión	television
la estantería	shelves
la cama	bed
el sofá	sofa
el escritorio	desk
el espejo	mirror

- **En mi dormitorio hay** In my bedroom there is
  una lámpara pero a lamp but
  no hay ordenador. there isn't a computer.
- **El ordenador está en** The computer is in
  el dormitorio de mi hermano. my brother's bedroom.

Where Things Are

- **Está…** It is…
  en in / on / at
  sobre on top of
  debajo de under
  al lado de next to
  detrás de behind
  delante de in front of
  entre between
- **En mi dormitorio,** In my bedroom,
  mi lámpara está my lamp is
  al lado del ordenador. next to the computer.

Key Point

To explain where something is we use the verb **estar**:

El armario está en mi dormitorio.

The wardrobe is in my bedroom.

Key Point

If the word after **de** is masculine **(el)** use **del**:

Mi televisión está al lado del armario.

My television is next to the wardrobe.

Reminder: **de + el = del**
de + la = de la.

Activities at Home

- **veo**   I watch
  juego   I play
  escucho   I listen
  descanso   I relax
  trabajo   I work
- **Trabajo en mi dormitorio.**   I work in my bedroom.

Chores

- **Arreglo mi dormitorio.**   I tidy my bedroom.
- **Paso la aspiradora.**   I do the hoovering.
- **Ayudo a mi madre.**   I help my mum.
- **Cocino.**   I cook / I do the cooking.
- **Lavo los platos.**   I do the dishes.
- **Hago...**   I do...
  Hago la compra.   I do the shopping.
  Hago de canguro.   I babysit.
  Hago mi cama.   I make my bed.

How Often?

- **raramente**   rarely
  a menudo   often
  cada día   every day
  todos los días   every day
  a veces   sometimes
  una vez a la semana   once a week
  normalmente   usually
- **En casa raramente cocino**   At home I rarely cook
  sin embargo hago mi cama   however I make my
  a diario.   bed daily.

Negatives

- **no**   not
  No hago la compra.   I don't do the shopping.
- **no...nunca**   never
  No hago la compra nunca.   I never do the shopping.
- **Nunca hago la compra.**   I never do the shopping.
  no...nada   nothing
  No hago nada.   I do nothing.

Quick Test

1. What is the Spanish for these items: a desk, a bed, a chair and a computer?
2. Which items in question 1 are masculine? Which ones are feminine?
3. Write in Spanish that your desk is next to the wardrobe.
4. Say in Spanish that you help your mum every day.

Key Vocab	
al lado de	next to
hago	I do
en	in / on / at
en mi	in my
dormitorio...	bedroom...
está...	is / it is...

Food and Drink 1

You must be able to:

- Use the Spanish for fruits and vegetables
- Ask for drinks and snacks in a café
- Say how often you eat certain things and say what you like to eat.

Vegetables

- **unas patatas** — potatoes
- **una zanahoria** — carrot
- **un col** — cabbage
- **una cebolla** — onion
- **unos guisantes** — peas
- **una lechuga** — lettuce
- **un pimiento** — pepper
- **unos champiñones** — mushrooms

Fruit

- **una manzana** — apple
- **una pera** — pear
- **un limón** — lemon
- **un melocotón** — peach
- **un plátano** — banana
- **una fresa** — strawberry

Ordering Drinks and Snacks

- **Me gustaría... por favor.** — I would like... please.
- **Quisiera...** — I'd like...
- **un café con leche** — a white coffee
- **un café / té solo** — a black coffee / tea
- **un chocolate caliente** — a hot chocolate
- **una coca-cola** — a coca-cola
- **una limonada** — a lemonade
- **un agua mineral (con / sin gas)** — a (fizzy / still) mineral water
- **un zumo de naranja** — an orange juice
- **un bocadillo de jamón y queso** — a ham and cheese sandwich
- **una tortilla española** — Spanish omelette
- **unos calamares** — squid
- **una paella de mariscos** — seafood paella
- **una ensalada mixta** — a mixed salad

Key Point

Note how to specify what you would like:

un café	a coffee
con leche	with milk
un bocadillo de atún	a tuna sandwich
un sándwich de atún	a toasted tuna sandwich

Likes and Dislikes

- **Como frescas porque
  me gusta el sabor.**
  I eat strawberries because
  I like the taste.
- **Como mucha ensalada
  porque es buena para la
  salud.**
  I eat lots of salad
  because it is good for your health.
- **No me gustan las cebollas
  porque no me gusta el olor.**
  I don't like onions
  because I don't like the smell.
- **Me gustan las patatas
  pero odio las peras.**
  I like potatoes
  but I hate pears.

> ### Key Point
>
> Note how to talk about
> your likes and dislikes:
> **Me gusta**   I like
> **No me gusta**   I don't like
> **Odio**   I hate

How Often?

- **Bebo té cada día.**   I drink tea every day.
- **Rara vez bebo té.**   I rarely drink tea.
- **Como sandía de vez
  en cuando.**   I eat watermelon now
                                   and then.
- **a menudo**   often
  cada día / todos los días   every day
  a veces   sometimes
  dos veces a la semana   twice a week
  normalmente   usually
  diariamente   daily

> ### Key Point
>
> To say I am hungry and I
> am thirsty you use the verb
> **tener** (to have) and not
> **ser** (to be):
> **Tengo hambre.**   I am
>   hungry.
> **Tengo sed.**   I am
>   thirsty.

> ### Key Vocab
>
> | | |
> |---|---|
> | **rara vez** | rarely |
> | **me gustaría** | I would |
> | **quisiera** | like |
> | **como** | I eat |
> | **bebo** | I drink |
> | **(no) me gusta** | I (don't) |
> | | like |
> | **cada día** | every day |
> | **todos los días** | every day |
> | **a veces** | sometimes |
> | **a menudo** | often |
> | **de vez en** | now and |
> | **cuando** | then |

> ### Quick Test
>
> 1. Which is the odd one out?
>   a) una cebolla   b) un melocotón
>   c) una zanahoria   d) una patata
> 2. Translate the following into Spanish: I eat apples every day.
> 3. Translate the following into English:
>   Como sandía porque me gusta el sabor.
> 4. Which sentence is not true?
>   a) Los plátanos son amarillos.
>   b) Las fresas son rojas.
>   c) Los guisantes son negros.

Food and Drink 2

You must be able to:

- Understand a menu
- Order a meal in a restaurant
- Follow a simple recipe.

First Course

- **las entradas** — starters
  la sopa de verduras — vegetable soup
  la ensalada mixta — mixed salad
  el gazpacho — cold vegetable soup
  la tortilla española — Spanish omelette

Main Course

- **los platos principales** — mains / main courses
  el pollo — chicken
  el pescado — fish
  el bistec — steak
  las albóndigas — meatballs
  la carne de vaca / cerdo — beef / pork
  el cordero — lamb
  los mariscos — seafood
  las gambas — prawns
  la paella de mariscos — seafood paella

And Finally

- **Me gustaría... por favor.** — I would like… please.
- **los postres** — desserts / puddings
  un helado — an ice cream
  el arroz con leche — rice pudding
  el flan — creme caramel
  la tarta de chocolate — chocolate cake

Ordering a Meal

- **¿Tiene una mesa para dos personas?** — Do you have a table for two people?
- **Quisiera... por favor.** — I'd like… please.
- **Quiero...** — I want…
- **De primero he elegido...** — For a starter, I've chosen…
- **Para beber...** — To drink…
- **La carta, por favor.** — The menu, please.

Key Point

In a restaurant, you speak to the waiter or waitress using the **usted** form of the verb to be polite:

¿Tiene una mesa para cinco personas?

Do you have a table for five people?

Key Point

Note the words for 'some':
unos postres (masculine)
some desserts
unas tartas (feminine)
some cakes

After a quantity use **de**:
un kilo de patatas

¿Dónde están los servicios?	Where are the toilets?
¿Qué recomienda?	What do you recommend?
la cuenta	the bill
El servicio está incluido.	Service is included.
una propina	a tip

Following a Recipe

añadir / agregar	add
calentar	heat up
batir	beat / whisk
revolver	stir
ajustar	adjust
servir	serve

Chocolate Caliente: Spanish Hot Chocolate

los ingredientes para 2 tazas	ingredients for 2 cups
450 mililitros de leche entera	450 ml whole milk
70 gramos de chocolate (70% cacao finamente picado)	70 g chocolate (70% cocoa finely chopped)
30 gramos de chocolate con leche (de buena calidad finamente picado)	30 g milk chocolate (good quality finely chopped)
75 mililitros de nata líquida	75 ml single cream
¼ cucharadita de canela molida	¼ tsp ground cinammon
una pizca de sal	a pinch of salt

El Método: The Method

Calentar 150 mililitros de leche en una cacerola a fuego medio.	Heat up 150 ml of milk in a saucepan on a medium heat.
Añadir el chocolate y revolver hasta que se derrita.	Add the chocolate and stir until it melts.
Agregar la leche y nata.	Add the rest of the milk and cream.
Añadir la sal y la canela.	Add the salt and the cinnamon.
Ajustar al sabor.	Adjust to taste.
Batir antes de servir.	Whisk before serving.

Quick Test

1. Which is not a dessert?
   a) una tarta de queso   b) un helado de vainilla
   c) una ensalada de fruta   d) una ensalada mixta
2. Translate the following into Spanish:
   For dessert, I would like a strawberry ice cream.
3. Translate the following into English:
   Añadir un poco de azúcar al café.

Key Vocab

¿Tiene...?	Do you have...?
Quisiera...	I'd like...
Quiero...	I want...
he elegido	I have chosen

Sport and Health 1

You must be able to:

- Recognise sports in Spanish
- Talk about what sports you like
- Say how often you do sports.

Sports and Games

el fútbol	football
el tenis	tennis
el ajedrez	chess
el baloncesto	basketball
el bádminton	badminton
el rugby	rugby
los juegos de mesa	board games
las cartas	cards
la pelota	Basque pelota (handball)
el billar	billiards
el hockey	hockey
el mini-golf	crazy golf

Key Point

When talking about sports and games **jugar** is followed by **al** or **a la**: **jugar al fútbol**, **jugar al tenis**, **jugar al baloncesto**, **jugar a las cartas**.

When talking about playing an instrument, use the verb **tocar**: **tocar el piano**, **tocar la guitarra**.

Likes and Dislikes

- You already know the expressions **me gusta**, **no me gusta** and **odio** so here are a few new phrases:

Me flipa el fútbol.	I'm crazy about football.
Me apasiona la pelota.	I'm crazy about Basque pelota.
Me encanta el rugby.	I love rugby. (Rugby enchants me.)
No soporto el baloncesto.	I can't stand basketball.
Me aburre el billar.	Billiards bores me.

How Often?

No juego al fútbol a menudo.	I don't play football often.
Juego al hockey una vez a la semana.	I play hockey once a week.
De vez en cuando toco el piano.	I play piano now and then.
No toco nunca la batería.	I never play the drums.

More Activities

- All of these activities use the verb **hacer** (to do):

hacer natación	to go swimming
hacer equitación	to go horse-riding
hacer ciclismo	to go cycling
hacer esquí	to go skiing
hacer vela	to go sailing
hacer patinaje sobre hielo	to go ice-skating
hacer patinaje sobre ruedas	to go roller-skating
hacer monopatín	to go skateboarding
hacer gimnasia	to do gymnastics
hacer atletismo	to do athletics
hacer deportes de riesgo	to do extreme sports
hacer footing	to go jogging
hacer boxeo	to do boxing
hacer deportes	to do / play sports

- **A mi hermana** le gusta **hacer vela.** — My sister likes to go sailing.

- **A mi padre** le encanta **hacer esquí acuático.** — My dad loves to go water-skiing.

- **Yo prefiero hacer natación.** — I prefer to go swimming.

Quick Test

1. Complete the sentence. Se puede hacer natación…
   a) al centro comercial.   b) en la piscina.
   c) en la estación.   d) al cine.
2. Translate the following into Spanish:
   I'm crazy about basketball but I can't stand football.
3. Translate the following into English:
   Juego al fútbol cada día, pero nunca toco la guitarra.
4. Which is the odd one out?
   a) las cartas   b) los juegos de mesa
   c) el billar   d) el patinaje

Key Vocab

le gusta	he / she likes
me apasiona	I am passionate about
le encanta	he / she loves
me encanta	I love (it enchants me)
me flipa	I'm crazy about
no soporto	I can't stand
me aburre	It bores me
yo prefiero	I prefer

Sport and Health 2

You must be able to:

- Say how you are feeling
- Talk about what is good and bad for you
- Talk about how you will stay healthy in the future.

Feeling Unwell

- **Estoy enfermo / enferma.**   I'm ill.
- **Estoy resfriado / resfriada.**   I have a cold.
- **Tengo tos.**   I have a cough.
- **Me duele la cabeza.**   I've got a headache. (My head hurts.)
- **Me duele la pierna.**   I've got a sore leg.
- **Me duele la garganta.**   I have a sore throat.
- **Me duele la espalda.**   I have a sore back.
- **Me duele el brazo.**   I have a sore arm.
- **Me duele el pie.**   I've got a sore foot.
- **Me duelen los dientes.**   I've got toothache. (My teeth hurt.)
- **Me duelen las orejas.**   I've got earache. (My ears hurt.)
- **Me duelen los ojos.**   I've got sore eyes.

> ### Key Point
>
> **You must use the definite** article after **me duele (singular):**
> **Me duele la cabeza.**
> I've got a headache. (My head hurts.)
> Plural words need to follow **me duelen (plural):**
> **Me duelen los dientes.**
> I've got toothache. (My teeth hurt).

Good or Bad for You

- **Es bueno / buena para la salud.**   It's good for you / your health.
- **Es malo / mala para la salud.**   It's bad for you / your health.
- **No como comida grasa, es mala para la salud.**   I don't eat greasy food, it's bad for you / your health.
- **Como fruta a menudo, es buena para la salud.**   I often eat fruit, it's good for you / your health.
- **No fumo, es malo para los pulmones.**   I don't smoke, it is bad for the lungs.
- **El azúcar es malo para los dientes.**   Sugar is bad for your teeth.
- **La fruta y las legumbres son buena para el corazón.**   Fruit and vegetables are good for the heart.

Staying Healthy

Quiero mantenerme en forma.	I want to stay fit.
Voy a comer mejor.	I'm going to eat better.
Voy a beber más agua.	I'm going to drink more water.
Voy a comer menos azúcar.	I'm going to eat less sugar.
No voy a fumar porque es malo para la salud.	I'm not going to smoke because it's bad for your health.
más verduras	more vegetables
menos hamburguesas	fewer hamburgers

Getting Help

el médico	the doctor
Voy a ir al médico.	I'm going to go to the doctor's.
el dentista	the dentist
Tengo una cita al dentista.	I have an appointment at the dentist's.
la farmacia	the chemist's
el hospital	the hospital

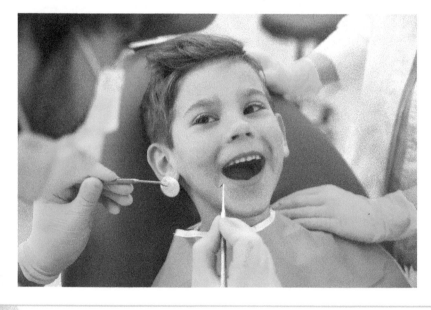

Revise

Key Point

The verb **ir a** is followed by an infinitive verb to form the near future tense.

Voy a comer más sano.
I'm going to eat more healthily.

Voy a beber menos gaseosa.
I am going to drink fewer fizzy drinks.

Key Vocab

estoy enfermo / enferma	I'm ill
me duele / duelen	I've got (a) sore…
es bueno / buena para la salud	It's good for your health
es malo / mala para la salud	It's bad for your health
tengo	I have
voy a	I'm going to
más	more
menos	less

Quick Test

1. Complete the sentence. **Me duelen…**
   a) la cabeza. b) el pie.
   c) la espalda. d) los dientes.
2. Translate the following into Spanish:
   I'm ill, I've got a sore throat and a headache.
3. Translate the following into English: **No como mucha comida grasa porque es mala para la salud.**
4. Which is not healthy?
   a) Voy a comer fruta. b) Voy a jugar al tenis.
   b) Voy a fumar. d) Voy a hacer la natación.

Review Questions

Use a separate piece of paper for your answers, if necessary.

KS2 Key Concepts

1 What colour do you get when you mix two colours together? Write the Spanish for each new colour from these combinations.

a) rojo + azul = ...   b) amarillo + azul = ...

c) negro + blanco = ...   d) rojo + blanco = ...   [4]

2 Count up to twenty in Spanish. Write the numbers down in words. [20]

3 What are the seven days of the week in Spanish? Write them down. [7]

4 Fill in the gaps with the missing months in Spanish.

enero	a)	marzo	b) ....
mayo	c)	julio	d) ....
septiembre	e)	noviembre	f) .... [6]

5 Write the answers to these sums.

a) uno + dos = ...   b) tres + cuatro = ...   c) cinco + siete = ...

d) veinte – seis = ...   e) tres × dos = ...   f) cinco × cuatro = ...

g) dieciséis – tres = ...   h) doce – ocho = ...   i) once – uno = ...

j) dos × nueve = ...   k) trece – dos = ...   l) diez + cinco = ...

[12

6 Match up the numbers.

veinticinco	79
treinta y siete	42
cuarenta y dos	83
setenta y nueve	37
ochenta y tres	25

[5

7 Write the following numbers in Spanish.

a) 29   b) 51   c) 72   d) 86   e) 94   [5

8 Fill in the gaps with the appropriate numbers to indicate what time it is.

a) 1:00   Es la _____.

b) 7:00   Son las _____.

c) 8:10   Son las ocho _____.

d) 10:15   Son las _____ y cuarto.

e) 11:30   Son las _____ y media.

f) 4:45   Son las _____ menos cuarto.

g) 6:55   Son las _____ menos cinco.   [7]

9 Write out the times. Use the examples in question **8** to help you.

a) 2:00   **b)** 3:20   **c)** 6:15

d) 9:30   **e)** 8:45   **f)** 11:50   [6]

10 Match the two halves to form a question.

¿Qué fecha	nació en septiembre?
¿Cuánto	tu cumpleaños?
¿Quién	en invierno?
¿Dónde hace calor	es hoy?
¿Cómo se dice	cuesta?
¿Cuándo es	'miércoles' en inglés?

[6]

11 Read the text and find the Spanish for each of the phrases below.

Hoy hace mucho calor en Barcelona y hay una temperatura de 30 grados. Hace sol por todo España. Hace muy buen tiempo también en el sur de Inglaterra, pero hace viento en el norte de Inglaterra. En Irlanda hace mal tiempo y llueve y hay una temperatura de 15 grados. En Escocia hace frío y en Gales hay niebla.

a) it is very hot   **b)** it is sunny   **c)** it is bad weather

d) it is raining   **e)** it is cold   **f)** it is windy

g) it is foggy   **h)** it is good weather   **i)** it is 30 degrees   [9]

Use a separate piece of paper for your answers, if necessary.

Family

1   Join up the questions to the appropriate answers.

¿Cómo te llamas?	Él se llama Felipe.
¿Cuántos años tienes?	Sí, tengo un perro.
¿Tienes hermanos?	No, soy hijo único.
¿Tienes mascotas?	Tengo trece años.
¿Cómo se llama tu padre?	Me llamo Ana.

[5]

2   Fill the gaps with the words provided in the box.

una   se llama   años   marrones   hermanos   castaño   cariñosos   gato

a)   Me llamo María y tengo doce _____.

b)   Tengo _____ hermana y dos _____.

c)   Tengo los ojos _____ y el pelo _____.

d)   Mis padres son _____.

e)   Tengo un _____ que _____ Pedro.   [8]

3   Look at the detail cards below and write down what the people would say about themselves in Spanish.

Name: Marco
Date of birth: 31.5.08
Address: Madrid
Siblings: none
Eyes: blue
Hair: short and black
Pets: none

Name: Elena
Date of birth: 11.7.09
Address: Mérida
Siblings: one sister and one brother
Eyes: green
Hair: long and brown
Pets: one rabbit, age three

[14]

House and Home

1 Translate the words below into Spanish and include the correct article: **el**, **la**, **un** or **una**.

a) the living room _____ **b)** the bedroom _____

c) the kitchen _____ **d)** the attic _____

e) the bathroom _____ **f)** the wardrobe _____

g) the bed _____ **h)** the chair _____

i) the desk _____ **j)** the computer _____ [10]

2 Match the two halves of the sentences below.

En mi dormitorio	**mi escritorio.**
La televisión está sobre	**en el salón.**
Comparto mi dormitorio	**hay un ordenador.**
Hay dos sillones	**con mi hermana.**

[4]

3 Fill in the gaps using the words below.

sur	dormitorio	en	diez	ciudad
hay	ordenador	apartamento	jardín	encanta

Vivo _____ **un** _____ **grande en una** _____ **pequeña**

en el _____ **de Inglaterra. Me** _____ **mi ciudad. En mi casa hay**

_____ **habitaciones, pero no hay** _____ **. En mi** _____

hay un _____ **. Es genial. En el dormitorio de mi hermano** _____ **una**

consola. [10]

Use a separate piece of paper for your answers, if necessary.

Food and Drink

1 Marco is talking about things he does and doesn't like to eat. Write down **three** things in English that he does eat.

No me gusta nada la fruta porque es horrible. Como muchas verduras, sobre todo la ensalada, pero no soporto las cebollas. A menudo como pollo porque es bueno para la salud, pero odio el pescado ya que no me gusta nada ni el sabor ni el olor. De postre prefiero un pastel de chocolate, pero detesto los helados porque son malsanos y lleno de azúcar.

[3]

2 Look at this menu and choose a starter, main course, dessert and a drink for Ana who is a vegetarian. Ana likes fruit but doesn't eat too much sugar.

Menu

Entradas
Sopa de tomate
Jamón Serrano con melón
Boquerones

Platos principales
Paella de mariscos
Lomo de cerdo
Tortilla española

Postres
Tarta de manzana
Helado de fresa
Macedonia de frutas

Bebidas
Limonada
Café al gusto
Té al gusto

[4

Sport and Health

1 What problem are these people describing? Choose the correct picture.

a) **Me duelen los dientes.**   b) **Me duele la cabeza.**   c) **Me duelen los pies.**

d) **Me duele la espalda.**   e) **Me duele el estómago.**

A

B

C

D

E

[5]

2 Identify the correct sport. Write your answer in Spanish.

Para hacer este deporte…

a) **se necesita un caballo.**   b) **se necesita una bicicleta.**   c) **se necesita una raqueta.**

_____   _____   _____

d) **se necesita un balón.**   e) **se necesita un barco.**

_____   _____

[5]

3 Put these words into two columns: **Bueno para la salud** (good for you) and **Malo para la salud** (bad for you).

a) **Las patata fritas**   b) **La ensalada**   c) **La natación**

d) **Las drogas**   e) **Los cigarillos**   f) **Los dulces**

g) **Las legumbres**   h) **El agua**   [8]

School and Education 1

You must be able to:

- Say what subjects you like and dislike and why
- Describe your school
- Talk about your school day.

School and Subjects

la escuela	(primary) school
el colegio	(high) school
el instituto	(high) school
la asignatura	subject
el inglés	English
el español	Spanish
el francés	French
el alemán	German
los idiomas	languages
las ciencias	science
la física	physics
la biología	biology
la química	chemistry
las matemáticas	maths
la informática	ICT (computing)
la tecnología	technology
la religión	RE / religious studies
el deporte	sport
la educación física	PE
la historia	history
la geografía	geography

Likes and Dislikes

- You already know the expressions **me gusta**, **no me gusta** and **odio** so here are a few new phrases:

Me mola el español.	I'm crazy about Spanish.
Mi asignatura favorita es el español.	My favourite subject is Spanish.
Detesto el deporte.	I detest sport.
Me aburren las matemáticas.	Maths bores me.

Giving Opinions

- Here are some useful activities to use when saying why you like or dislike a subject:

interesante	interesting
aburrido	boring
fácil	easy
difícil	difficult
divertido	fun
duro	hard
útil	useful
inútil	useless

- **Me gusta el español**   I like Spanish
  porque es interesante.   because it is interesting.
- **Me encanta la tecnología**   I love technology
  porque es útil.   because it is useful.
- **No me gusta la historia**   I don't like history
  porque es aburrida.   because it is boring.

Giving Reasons Why

- To give a reason why you like a subject, or not, you can use a phrase with a verb in it:

Me mola el español,	I'm crazy about Spanish,
porque el profe es fantástico.	because the teacher is fantastic.
No me gusta la geografía,	I don't like geography,
porque hay muchos deberes.	because there is lots of homework.

> ### Key Point
>
> When explaining why you like or dislike a subject, you must use the correct form of the adjective to agree with the subject you are describing:
>
> **El inglés es fantástico.**
> English is fantastic.
>
> **La historia es fantástica.**
> History is fantastic.

Quick Test

1. Which is the odd one out?
   a) el español   b) el inglés   c) la historia
2. Translate the following into Spanish: I like history because it is fun.
3. Translate the following into English: **No me gustan las matemáticas porque el profe es aburrido.**
4. Which sentence does not make sense?
   a) **Me gusta el dibujo, porque es creativo.**
   b) **Detesto la geografía porque es aburrida.**
   c) **Me encanta el inglés porque es inútil.**

> ### Key Vocab
>
> | | |
> |---|---|
> | **me mola** | I love |
> | **porque** | because |
> | **mi asignatura** | my |
> | **favorita** | favourite subject |
> | **detesto** | I detest / hate |
> | **me aburren** | they bore me |
> | **me gusta** | I like |
> | **no me gusta** | I don't like |

School and Education 2

You must be able to:

- Talk about a typical school day
- Describe your uniform
- Talk about school rules.

The School Day

Voy al colegio en autobús.	I go to school by bus.
Voy al colegio en coche.	I go to school by car.
Voy al colegio a pie.	I go to school on foot.
Las clases comienzan a las nueve.	Lessons start at 9 o'clock.
Hay un recreo de quince minutos.	There is a 15-minute break.
Hay cinco clases al día.	There are five lessons per day.
La hora de comer es a mediodía.	The lunch break is at midday.
Las clases terminan a las tres y media.	Classes finish at half-past three.

Describing your School

Mi colegio es grande / pequeño.	My school is big / small.
Los edificios son modernos.	The buildings are modern.
Los edificios son bastante viejos.	The buildings are quite old.

School Facilities

Hay...	There is / are...
una biblioteca	a library
una cantina	a canteen
unos laboratorios	laboratories
un patio	a playground
un campo de deportes	a sports field
un salón de actos	a hall
novecientos estudiantes	nine hundred students
mil alumnos	a thousand students
unos setenta profes	about seventy teachers

School Rules

- **Se puede** — you can
  No se puede — you can't
  Está permitido — you're allowed
  Está prohibido — it is forbidden
  Hay que — you must
- **Está prohibido utilizar** — It is forbidden to use
  el móvil en clase. — mobile phones in class.
- **Hay que llevar uniforme.** — You must wear uniform.
- **Llevar maquillaje** — Wearing make-up
  no está permitido. — is not permitted.

School Uniform

- **Mi uniforme es cómodo.** — My uniform is comfortable.
- **Es práctico, pero no me** — It's practical but I don't like the
  gustan ni el color ni el estilo. — colour or the style.
- **Hay que llevar...** — You must wear…
  unos pantalones — trousers
  una falda — a skirt
  zapatos negros — black shoes
  una corbata — a tie
  una camisa blanca — a white shirt
  una chaqueta roja — a red blazer
  un jersey gris — a grey jumper
- **Quisiera ir al colegio** — I'd like to go to school
  en España porque — in Spain because
  no hay uniforme y — there's no uniform and
  pienso que es guay. — I think that's cool.

Key Point

When describing uniform, make sure the colour agrees:

Llevo una falda negra y un jersey negro con unos pantalones negros. I wear a black skirt and a black jumper with black trousers.

Key Vocab

hay	there is / there are
hay que	you must
está	you're
permitido	allowed
está	it is
prohibido	forbidden
se puede	you can / one can
no se puede	you cannot / one cannot

Quick Test

1. Which is the odd one out?
   a) se puede   b) está prohibido   c) hay que
2. Translate the following into Spanish: You must wear a black jacket.
3. Translate the following into English:
   Las clases empiezan a las nueve y cuarto.
4. Which sentence does not make sense?
   a) Odio el uniforme porque es incómodo.
   b) Detesto el color porque es horrible.
   c) No me gusta el uniforme porque es cómodo.

Future Plans 1

You must be able to:

- Talk about jobs
- Talk about places of work
- Give opinions on work.

Jobs

- The ending of the word for some jobs changes depending on the gender it describes.

Él es enfermero.	He is a nurse.
Ella es enfermera.	She is a nurse.

- To describe what you want to be or what you would like to be in the future, use one of these phrases and add the noun for the job:

Quiero ser...	I want to be a / an...
Me gustaría ser...	I would like to be a / an...
Quisiera ser...	I'd like to be a / an...
Espero ser...	I hope to be a / an...
abogado / abogada	lawyer
actor / actriz	actor / actress
cantante	singer
contable	accountant
director / directora de una empresa	company director / manager
diseñador / diseñadora de videojuegos	games designer
diseñador / diseñadora web	web designer
enfermero / enfermera	nurse
entrenador / entrenadora	coach / trainer
futbolista	footballer
ingeniero / ingeniera	engineer
intérprete	interpreter
médico / médica	doctor
peluquero / peluquera	hairdresser
periodista	journalist
piloto	pilot
profesor / profesora	teacher
traductor / traductora	translator
veterinario / veterinaria	vet

Places of Work

-

Trabajo en...	I work in...
un aeropuerto	an airport
un colegio	a school
una fábrica	a factory

Key Point

When talking about what your job is or what your job is going to be, you don't need the word 'a'. For example: **Soy médico.** I am a doctor.

un hospital	a hospital
una oficina	an office
un teatro	a theatre
una tienda	a shop

Adjectives

- These adjectives describe personal attributes that are appropriate to the world of work:

apasionado / a	passionate
cortés	polite
enérgico / a	energetic
organizado / a	organised
paciente	patient
respetuoso / a	respectful
tolerante	tolerant
trabajador / a	hard-working

- These adjectives are useful for describing a job:

activo / a	active
bien pagado / a	well-paid
estimulante	stimulating
fascinante	fascinating
frustrante	frustrating
gratificante	rewarding
motivador / a	motivating

Verbs

- Use some of these together with the modal verbs:

compartir	to share
comunicarse	to communicate
cooperar	to cooperate
coordinar	to coordinate
crear	to create
inventar	to invent
trabajar solo / a	to work alone
trabajar en equipo	to work in a team

As an alternative to modal verbs use **hay que**:

Hay que comunicar.	You must / It is necessary to communicate.
Hay que ser trabajador / a.	You must / It is necessary to be hard-working.

> ### Key Point
>
> Modal verbs are followed by an infinitive. For example:
>
> **Quiero inventar.**
> I want to invent.
>
> **Debo compartir.**
> I must share.
>
> **Puedo comunicarme.**
> I can communicate.

Quick Test

1. Name three jobs that change according to gender.
2. Where would '**un enfermero**' work?
3. Who might work '**en una oficina**'?
4. How would you translate '**Hay que trabajar**'?

> ### Key Vocab
>
> | | |
> |---|---|
> | **hay que** | It is necessary / You must |
> | **puedo** | I can / am able to |
> | **debo** | I must |
> | **espero** | I hope |

Future Plans 2

You must be able to:

- Talk about your priorities
- Use appropriate future time phrases
- Talk about future study
- Talk about ambitions.

Priorities

- Try to relate your future plans to what is important to you.
- **Es esencial.**   It's essential.
- **Es imprescindible.**   It's essential.
- **Es necesario.**   It's necessary.
- **Lo que es importante**   What's important
  para mí es…   for me is…
  mi familia   my family
  la salud   my health
  mis amigos   my friends
  mis estudios   my studies
  el dinero   money
  la felicidad   happiness
  el planeta   the planet
  el éxito   success

Key Point

Es can easily be made negative:

No es it's not

Ya no es it's no longer

Time Phrases

- **En primer lugar**   First of all
- **después**   next / after that
- **luego**   then
- **en el futuro**   in the future
- **en tres años**   in three years
- **el año próximo**   next year
- **el año que viene**   next year
- **cuando deje el colegio**   when I leave school

Study

- To talk about what you are going to do, use the near future tense:
  ir a + infinitive.
  Voy a aprobar mis exámenes.   I'm going to pass my exams.
  Voy a dejar el colegio.   I'm going to leave school.
  Voy a estudiar.   I'm going to study.
  Voy a continuar mis estudios.   I'm going to continue my studies.
  Voy a ir a la universidad.   I'm going to go to university.
  Voy a hacer un aprendizaje.   I'm going to do an apprenticeship.
  Voy a buscar un empleo.   I'm going to look for a job.

Reasons Why

- You can use the following phrases to describe the reasons why you will choose to study certain subjects.

Soy fuerte en…	I am good at…
Soy débil en…	I'm no good at…
Me interesa(n)…	I'm interested in…
No me interesa(n)…	I'm not interested in…
Ya no me interesa(n)…	I'm no longer interested in…
Me apasiona(n)…	I'm passionate about…
Odio	I hate
Me aburre(n)…	I'm bored by…
Me flipa(n)…	I'm crazy about…
Soy hincho / hincha de…	I'm a fan of…

Key Point

The ability to move between the simple future tense and the near future tense could gain you marks in an assessment.

No es imprescindible.
It's not essential.

Ya no es necesario.
It's not necessary.

Ambitions: Simple Future Tense

Cuando tenga… años…	When I am… years old…
Hablaré dos idiomas.	I will speak two languages.
Seré famoso / famosa.	I will be famous.
Tendré éxito.	I will be successful.
Trabajaré en el extranjero.	I will work abroad.
Ganaré mucho dinero.	I will earn lots of money.
Viviré en una casa grande.	I will live in a big house.
Viajaré.	I will travel.
Viajaré alrededor del mundo.	I will travel around the world.
Ayudaré a otras personas.	I will help others.
Me enamoraré.	I will fall in love.
Me casaré.	I will get married.
Tendré hijos.	I will have children.
Seré feliz.	I will be happy.

Quick Test

1. Give two examples of ways to say you like / are good at a subject.
2. What are this person's priorities?
   Para mí, la salud y los amigos son imprescindibles.
3. Translate the following into English:
   Voy a estudiar matemáticas.
4. Complete this sentence: **Cuando tenga veintisiete años…**

Key Vocab

buscar	to look for
continuar	to continue
dejar	to leave
estudiar	to study
hacer	to do
ir	to go

Leisure 1

You must be able to:

- Name musical instruments
- Use the verb **tocar** + instruments
- Give your opinion on music.

Music

- **los instrumentos musicales**   musical instruments
  el piano   piano
  el violín   violin
  la viola   viola
  el clarinete   clarinet
  la flauta   flute
  la guitarra   guitar
  la batería   drums
  la trompeta   trumpet

> ### Key Point
>
> In Spanish, you use **tocar** to play an instrument but **jugar** to play a sport.
> For example:
> **Toco la trompeta y juego al rugby.**
> I play the trumpet and I play rugby.

Playing an Instrument

- **tocar**   to play (an instrument)
- **¿Tocas un instrumento?**   Do you play an instrument?
- **Sí, toco la flauta.**   Yes, I play the flute.
- **No, no toco ningún instrumento.**   No, I don't play an instrument.
- **No toco ningún instrumento pero me gustaría tocar la guitarra.**   I don't play an instrument but I would like to play the guitar.
- **No toco el piano porque creo que es muy difícil.**   I don't play the piano because I think it's very difficult.
- **Mi hermano toca la batería.**   My brother plays the drums.
- **Mi madre y yo tocamos el piano.**   My mum and I play the piano.

Types of Music

me gusta	I like
me encanta	I love
prefiero	I prefer
no soporto	I can't stand
Me interesa la música.	I'm interested in music.
Me encanta escuchar…	I love listening to…
No me gusta escuchar…	I don't like listening to…
la música pop	pop music
el jazz	jazz
el rock	rock music
la música clásica	classical music
música en vivo	live music

My Favourite

Mi cantante **favorito es…**	My favourite singer is…
Mi grupo **favorito es…**	My favourite group is…
Mi música favorita es la música clásica porque es relajante.	My favourite music is classical music because it's relaxing.

Adjectives

entretenido	entertaining
genial	great
animado	lively
lento	slow
rápido	fast
rítmico	rhythmic
relajante	relaxing

Key Vocab

el / la cantante	singer
entretenido	entertaining
el grupo	group
tocar	to play an instrument

Leisure 2

You must be able to:

- Name places in town and say where you go
- Use **al** or **a la** for 'to the' and **en** for 'in / at'
- Arrange to go to the cinema.

Places in the Town

- **el restaurante**   restaurant
  el cine   cinema
  el polideportivo   sports centre
  el club de jóvenes   youth club
  el centro comercial   shopping centre
  el teatro   theatre
  el parque   park
  la biblioteca   library
  la piscina   swimming pool
  la bolera   bowling alley
  la pista de patinaje   ice rink

> **Key Point**
>
> **Al / A la** means 'to the'.
>
> **En** means 'in' or 'at'.
>
> Don't forget to use the verb **estar** (to be) when talking about location, i.e. **Estoy en Londres**, not **Soy en Londres.**

At and To

- If you want to say 'to the' you need to use the preposition **'a'** followed by the definite article:

  a + el = al

  a + la = a la
- **Voy al gimnasio.**   I am going to the gym.
- **Vamos a la bolera.**   We are going to the bowling alley.
- To say you 'are in / at' a place use **en**:
- **Estoy en la biblioteca.**   I am in the library.
- **Estamos en el estadio de fútbol.**   We are at the football stadium.

Suggesting Where to Go

- ¿Vamos al / a la...?   Let's go to... / Shall we go to...?
- ¿Quieres ir al / a la...?   Do you want to go to...?
- ¿Te apetece ir al / a la...?   Do you fancy going to...?

Going to the Cinema

- una película **de acción**   an action film
  una película **policiaca**   a detective film
  una película **de ciencia ficción**   a sci-fi film
  una película **romántica**   a romantic film
  una **comedia**   a comedy
  un **dibujo animado**   a cartoon

Making Arrangements

- **¿Quieres ver una película en el cine?**   Do you want to see a film at the cinema?
- **¿Qué película ponen?**   What film is on?
- **Sí, es una buena idea.**   Yes, it's a good idea.
- **Sí, me encantaría ir.**   Yes, I would love to go.
- **¿A qué hora empieza?**   What time does it start?

Quick Test

1. Masculine or feminine? **parque / playa / centro comercial / biblioteca.**
2. Fill in with **al** or **a la**:
   a) Vamos _____ cine
   b) Voy _____ concierto
   c) ¿Quieres ir _____ bolera?
3. Ask someone in Spanish if they want to see a film tomorrow.
4. Name the genre of these films:
   a) *Dunkirk*
   b) *Happy Feet*
   c) *Star Wars*

Key Vocab

¿Quieres ir al / a la...?	Do you want to go to the...?
¿Te apetece ir al / a la...?	Do you fancy going to the...?
una película	a film
¿Vamos al / a la...?	Let's go to the...?

TV and Technology 1

You must be able to:

- Talk about which programmes you like and why
- Say how often you watch TV
- Use a range of adjectives and intensifiers.

TV Programmes

un dibujo animado	cartoon
un documental	documentary
un programa de telerrealidad	TV reality show
una emisión de deportes	a sports programme
un concurso	game show
una telenovela	soap
una serie de Netflix	a series on Netflix
las noticias	the news

Key Point

Mirar is to watch (**Miro** – I watch).
Ver is to see (**Veo** – I see) but in Spanish it is more common to say **Veo la televisión** – I watch TV.

Ver (to watch / see)

Veo la televisión.	I watch TV.
Veo una emisión de deportes.	I am watching a sports programme.
Prefiero ver los documentales.	I prefer to see / watch documentaries.
No veo las noticias.	I don't watch the news.
No me gusta ver la tele.	I don't like watching TV.
¿Te gusta ver los dibujos animados?	Do you like to watch cartoons?

How Often?

siempre	always
a menudo	often
de vez en cuando	from time to time
raramente	rarely
nunca	never
una vez al día	once a day
dos veces a la semana	twice a week

Adjectives

emocionante	exciting
fascinante	fascinating
impresionante	impressive
gracioso	funny
entretenido	entertaining
monótono	boring / monotonous
decepcionante	disappointing
tonto	silly
repetitivo	repetitive
informativo	informative

> **Key Point**
>
> **Se puede** – you can / one can.
> The verb after this has to be in the infinitive, i.e. **Se puede ver vídeos** – you can watch videos.

Examples of Sentences

- **A menudo veo los documentales sobre animales; me encantan porque son informativos.**
  I often watch animal documentaries; I love them because they are informative.

- **Mi hermana ve las telenovelas, pero no me gustan porque son tontas.**
  My sister watches soaps, but I don't like them because they are silly.

> **Quick Test**
>
> 1. Fill in the gaps: **Me gustan las** _____ **de ciencia ficción porque** _____ **impresionantes.**
> 2. Translate the following into Spanish: I never watch music programmes.
> 3. Translate the following into Spanish: I like soaps because they are exciting.
> 4. Change the verb **ver** into the 'I' and 'we' form.

TV and Technology 2

You must be able to:

- Say what you use your mobile phone for
- Talk about the positive and negative aspects of technology.

Online Activities

Mando mensajes.	I send messages.
Chateo con mis amigos.	I chat with friends.
Compruebo mis correos electrónicos.	I check my emails.
Juego a los videojuegos.	I play video games.
Hago cursos escolares en línea.	I do online classes.
Descargo música.	I download music.
Hago compras en línea.	I do online shopping.
Veo vídeos.	I watch videos.
Leo blogs.	I read blogs.
Comparto fotos.	I share photos.
Busco información.	I look for information.
Pongo mi página al día.	I update my page.
Organizo las salidas.	I make social arrangements.

Using Two-verb Phrases or Modal Verbs

- Don't forget that after certain verbs the second verb in the sentence stays in the infinitive. Learning the infinitive of each new verb is very important. Examples:

Quiero compartir fotos.	I want to share photos.
Me gusta descargar música.	I like to download music.
Puedo chatear con mis amigos.	I can chat with my friends.
Debo comprobar mis correos electrónicos.	I should check my emails.

> ### Key Point
>
> Putting the infinitive of regular verbs into the first person present tense is easy! Examples:
> **mandar – mando**
> **descargar – descargo**
> Be aware of irregulars, such as:
> **comprobar – compruebo**
> **jugar – juego**
> **hacer – hago**
> **poner – pongo**
> In the grammar section you will learn more about how these irregular verbs change.

Advantages of Technology

- **Me ayuda con mis estudios.** It helps me with my studies.
- **Se puede hacer cursos en casa.** You can do courses at home.
- **Se puede comunicar con personas en otros países fácilmente.** You can contact people in different countries easily.
- **Puedo estar en contacto con mis amigos.** I can be in contact with my friends.
- **Puedo estar al día con las noticias.** I can keep up to date with the news.
- **Puedo grabar momentos especiales.** I can record special moments.

Dangers of Technology

- **Es una distracción.** It's a distraction.
- **Puede ser una pérdida de tiempo.** It can be a waste of time.
- **Hay mucha violencia.** There's a lot of violence.
- **Hay mucho ciberacoso.** There's a lot of cyber bullying.
- **Hay demasiadas noticias falsas.** There's too much fake news.
- **Se puede encontrar personas peligrosas.** You can come across dangerous people.

Quick Test

1. What does **se puede** mean?
2. Fill in the gaps: **Es peligroso porque creo que** _____ **mucho** _____.
3. Change these verbs into the first person: **chatear, hacer, jugar.**
4. Unravel this sentence:
   noticias son veo siempre las porque informativas.

Key Vocab

chatear	to chat online
comprobar	to check
descargar	to download
estar al día	to be up to date
estar en contacto	to be in contact
grabar	to record

Review Questions

Use a separate piece of paper for your answers, if necessary.

Family

1 Who is it?

a) La madre de mi hermano, es .... b) El hermano de mi padre, es ....

c) El padre de mi padre, es .... d) La madre de mi madre, es ....

e) La hermana de mi hermano, es .... [5]

2 Match the two halves of each sentence and translate into English (below).

Tengo el pelo		alta y delgada.
Soy		trece años.
Tengo		azules.
Tengo los ojos		rubio.

[4]

a) ....

b) ....

c) ....

d) .... [4]

3 Sara is being asked about herself. Write a question for each of these answers.

a) Me llamo Sara. ....

b) Tengo catorce años. ....

c) El diecinueve de junio. ....

d) No, soy hija única. ....

e) Vivo en Alicante. ....

f) Sí, tengo un perro que se llama Rita. .... [6]

4 Fill in the gaps to complete the text.

Me _____ Alison. _____ doce años, pero mi hermana

_____ ocho años. Tengo el _____ largo y los

marrones. No tengo _____. Mi gato _____ Pedro. [7]

5 Translate into Spanish.

a) I am fifteen.

b) My birthday is on the sixth of May.

c) I have short blond hair and green eyes.

d) I have a white rabbit. [4]

House and Home

1 Fill in the gaps with **en**, **en un** or **en una**.

a) Vivo _____ Londres.

b) Vivimos _____ el norte de Inglaterra.

c) Mi amiga vive _____ casa grande.

d) Mis primos viven _____ apartamento. [4]

2 Put the words in the correct order to form sentences.

a) una   casa   en   vivo   pequeña

b) hay   casa   ocho   mi   en   habitaciones

c) ordenador   no   tengo   dormitorio   mi   en

d) televisor   está   la   sobre   mesa   el [4]

3 Make these sentences negative using **no**.

a) Tengo un ordenador.

b) Mi dormitorio es grande.

c) Tenemos un jardín.

d) Lavo los platos a menudo.

e) Mi hermana tiene un portátil en su dormitorio. [5]

4 Translate into Spanish.

a) I live in a small house in the South of England.

b) At home we have nine rooms.

c) I often do the vacuuming.

d) I do the washing up often, but it is boring. [4]

Use a separate piece of paper for your answers, if necessary.

Food and Drink

1 Find the fruit in each set of words.

a) una fresa   una zanahoria   unos guisantes

b) una patata   un limón   unos champiñones

c) una coliflor   un pimiento   un melocotón

d) una cebolla   una piña   un calabacín

e) unas judías   una manzana   una berenjena   [5]

2 Complete each sentence by choosing the correct words.

a) **Tomo la sopa de** ....

    melón.   **tomate.**   **calamares.**

b) **De postre he elegido** ....

    un helado.   **una tortilla.**   **paella.**

c) **Para beber voy a tomar** ....

    una manzana.   **un zumo de fruta.**   **una sopa.**

d) **¿Dónde están** ....

    la mesa?   **la cuenta?**   **los aseos?**   [4

3 Put the following words into one of four categories.

carne (meat)   **verduras** (vegetables)   **postres** (desserts)   **fruta** (fruit)

a) **unos champiñones**   b) **las peras**

c) **una tarta de fresa**   d) **unas albóndigas**

e) **un filete**   f) **unos plátanos**

g) **un helado de limón**   h) **unos guisantes**   [8

Sport and Health

1 Jemima is talking about how often she does different sports. Put the five sports in order from the one she does most often to the one she never does.

a) **De vez en cuando juego al hockey, una o dos veces al mes.**

b) **Hago natación una vez a la semana.**

c) **Juego al baloncesto dos veces a la semana.**

d) **No juego nunca al tenis.**

e) **Hago ciclismo cada día.**

.... [5]

2 Complete each sentence by choosing the correct ending.

a) **No como nunca helado porque** ....

    me gusta el sabor.   **es bueno para la salud.**   **es malo para la salud.**

b) **Hago deporte muy a menudo porque** ....

    quiero mantenerme en forma.   **es aburrido.**   **no soy deportista.**

c) **Voy al dentista porque** ....

    tengo dolor de pie.   **tengo dolor de cabeza.**   **me duelen los dientes.**   [3]

3 You are giving advice on how to stay healthy. Write **hay que** or **no hay que** in front of the following expressions.

a) .... **tomar ensalada.**

b) .... **beber agua.**

c) .... **comer mucho chocolate.**

d) .... **beber mucho café.**

e) .... **hacer deporte.**   [5]

Use a separate piece of paper for your answers, if necessary.

School and Education

 1 How do these people get to school? Choose the correct picture.

A

B

C

D

E

F

a) **Voy al colegio a pie.** ....

b) **Mis amigos y yo vamos al colegio en autobús.** ....

c) **Mi madre me lleva al colegio en coche.** ....

d) **Todos los días monto en bici para llegar al colegio.** .... [4]

2 Choose the answer which fits best.

a) **Me encanta el español porque es** ....

    aburrido   **difícil**   **útil**

b) **Me gusta la geografía porque el profe es** ....

    estricto   **genial**   **inútil**

c) **No me gusta nada la biología porque es** ....

    divertido   **súper**   **difícil**

d) **Odio la educación física porque soy** ....

    débil en deporte   **fuerte en deporte**   **deportista** [4]

Future Plans

1 Label the following images with the correct job title.

a)   b)   c)   d)

....   **[4]**

2 Sort the following words into the correct column in the table.

peluquero	ingeniera	médica	mujer de negocios	peluquera
cantante	actor	abogada	hombre de negocios	médico
	actriz	cantante	abogado	ingeniero

Masculine	Feminine

[14]

3 Choose the correct word to complete each sentence.

emocionante	rico	cortés

a) **Quisiera ser enfermero, pero hay que ser** ....

b) **Quiero ser piloto de fórmula uno porque sería** ....

c) **Voy a ser tenista porque quiero ser** ....   **[3]**

4 Describe your ambitions.

a) **En dos años…** ....

b) **En cinco años…** ....

c) **En diez años…** ....   **[6]**

Use a separate piece of paper for your answers, if necessary.

Leisure

1 Fill in the gaps with **al / a la**.

a) **Voy** .... **playa.**

b) **Vamos** .... **centro comercial.**

c) **Mi amigo va** .... **parque.**

d) **Me gusta ir** .... **pista de patinaje.** [4]

2 Read the paragragh and place the words in the correct gaps.

animados	tontas	Dumbo	padres	trece	telenovelas

Hola, me llamo Suki y tengo .... **años. Me encantan los dibujos**

.... **. Mi película favorita se llama** .... **. Veo las películas**

en casa con mis .... **. No me interesan las** .... **porque son**

.... **.** [6]

3 Look at the jumbled-up dialogue and then put the sentences in the correct order.

a) **¿Qué ponen?**

b) **A las cuatro y media.**

c) **¡Muy bien! Nos vemos en el cine.**

d) **¿Quieres ir al cine el sábado?**

e) **Ponen una película de Disney.**

f) **¿A qué hora empieza la película?** [6]

4 Look at these details and use them to make up a dialogue similar to the one in question 3.

When – Sunday

Film – *Toy Story 2*

Start time – 5 pm [6]

TV and Technology

1 Look at the sentences and decide which infinitive verb fits best.

a) V _____ vídeos   b) C _____ con mis amigos   c) D _____ música

d) B _____ información   e) L _____ blogs   f) J _____ videojuegos   [6]

2 Label the parts of the sentence with the grammatical terms below.

Siempre veo los documentales sobre los animales porque son muy impresionantes.

a) verb   b) adjective   c) noun

d) connective   e) intensifier   [7]

3 Answer the question in Spanish. Make sure you give a reason!

¿Cuál es tu programa favorito y por qué?

Start your answer with '**Mi programa favorito es**'.

_____   [2]

4 In Spanish, name **two** disadvantages of the Internet.

_____

_____   [2]

5 Write these sentences in Spanish.

a) I always chat with my friends.

_____

b) I often send messages to my friends in other countries.

_____

c) I sometimes download my favourite music.

_____

d) I love to watch sci-fi films with my brother.

_____   [4]

Shopping and Money 1

You must be able to:

- Describe clothes
- Ask and answer questions in a clothes shop.

Saying 'to wear'

- **Llevo.** — I wear.
- **Me gusta llevar.** — I like to wear.
- **Me gustaría llevar.** — I would like to wear.

> ### Key Point
>
> **La ropa** means clothes; you cannot say **las ropas**! E.g. **la ropa es bonita** – the clothes are nice / the clothing is nice.

Clothes

- la ropa — clothing / clothes
- **un jersey** — a jumper
- **un vestido** — a dress
- **un abrigo** — a coat
- **una camiseta** — a T-shirt
- **una camisa** — a shirt
- **una sudadera** — a sweatshirt
- **una gorra** — a cap
- **una falda** — a skirt
- **una chaqueta** — a jacket
- **una corbata** — a tie
- **unos pantalones** — trousers
- **unos vaqueros** — jeans
- **unos zapatos** — shoes
- **unas botas** — boots
- **unas zapatillas de deporte** — trainers

Descriptions

- de moda — fashionable
- **fuera de moda** — out of fashion
- **de algodón** — cotton
- **de lana** — woollen
- **de cuero** — leather
- **de rayas** — striped
- **de cuadros** — checked
- **de lunares** — polka dots
- **bonito** — pretty
- **feo** — ugly
- caro — expensive
- barato — cheap

- **unos vaqueros azules**   blue jeans
- **una camisa blanca**   white shirt
- Note the order when describing clothing – colour then fabric / pattern:
  un vestido rojo de algodón   a red cotton dress
  una chaqueta gris y negra de rayas   a grey and black striped jacket

Saying 'this' and 'these'

- Use **este / esta / estos / estas**.
- **Me gusta este jersey.**   I like this jumper.
  (masc. singuar)
- **Me encanta esta camisa.**   I like this shirt.
  (fem. singular)
- **Prefiero estos zapatos.**   I prefer these shoes.
  (masc. plural)
- **Estas botas son caras.**   These boots are expensive.
  (fem. plural)

Buying Clothes

- **¿En qué puedo servirle?**   How can I help you?
- **Quiero comprar esta chaqueta.**   I want to buy this jacket.
- **¿Qué talla?**   What size? (clothing)
- **¿Qué número?**   What size? (shoes)
- **¿De qué color?**   What colour?
- **Prefiero el azul.**   I prefer blue.
- **Quiero probar esta falda.**   I want to try on this skirt.
- **¿Cuánto es?**   How much is it?
- **Cuesta 40 Euros.**   It costs 40 Euros.

Key Vocab

barato	cheap
caro	expensive
¿Cuánto es?	How much is it?
de moda	fashionable
la ropa	clothes
llevar	to wear
probar	to try on

Shopping and Money 2

You must be able to:

- Talk about the pocket money you receive and what you spend it on
- Talk about household chores and jobs you do to earn money.

Pocket Money

- **Recibo… libras esterlinas**   I get £…
  … cada semana.   … every week.
  … cada mes.   … every month.
- **No recibo dinero de bolsillo.**   I don't get pocket money.
- **Gano mi dinero de bolsillo.**   I earn my pocket money.
- **Tengo que ganar…**   I have to earn…

Household Chores

- **Hago la compra.**   I do the shopping.
- **Ayudo en casa.**   I help at home.
- **Cuido a mi hermano menor.**   I look after my younger brother.
- **Trabajo en el jardín.**   I do gardening.
- **Preparo la comida.**   I prepare meals.
- **Lavo los platos.**   I wash the dishes.
- **Arreglo mi dormitorio.**   I tidy my room.
- **Pongo la mesa.**   I lay the table.
- **Paseo al perro.**   I walk the dog.
- **No hago nada.**   I don't do anything.

Spending Money

- **Gasto mi dinero en…**   I spend my money on…
  … ropa, videojuegos, libros, revistas, maquillaje, caramelos   … clothes, videogames, books, magazines, make-up, sweets
- **Suelo comprar…**   I usually buy…
- **Ahorro mi dinero.**   I save my money.

Part-time Jobs

- **Tengo un trabajo.**   I have a job.
- **Trabajo a tiempo parcial.**   I work part-time.
- **Reparto periódicos.**   I deliver newspapers.
- **Hago de canguro.**   I babysit.
- **Trabajo para mi tío.**   I work for my uncle.
- **Mi hermana mayor trabaja en una tienda.**   My older sister works in a shop.
- **Mi primo trabaja en un restaurante.**   My cousin works in a restaurant.
- **Me gustaría trabajar en una peluquería.**   I would like to work in a hairdresser's.
- **Trabajo en mis vacaciones.**   I work in my holidays.

Describing your Job

- **Empiezo a las nueve.**   I start at 9 o'clock.
- **Termino a las cinco.**   I finish at 5 o'clock.
- **Gano ocho libras por hora.**   I earn £8 an hour.
- **Me gustaría ganar 50 libras al día.**   I would like to earn £50 a day.
- **Me gusta mucho mi trabajo.**   I really like my job.

Key Vocab

dinero de bolsillo	pocket money
libras esterlinas	pounds (£)
recibir	to receive / get

Where I Live 1

You must be able to:

- Recognise places in a town
- Describe where you live and give simple directions
- Talk about the differences between the town and the country.

Places in a Town

el pueblo	town / village
el cine	cinema
el museo	museum
el parque	park
el polideportivo	sports centre
el estadio	stadium
el centro comercial	shopping centre
el mercado	market
el ayuntamiento	town hall
la biblioteca	library
la iglesia	church
la piscina	swimming pool
la tienda	shop
la ciudad	city / town
la plaza	town square

Key Point

el (masc.) and **la** (fem.) both mean 'the'.

un (masc.) and **una** (fem.) mean 'a', e.g.
el banco – the bank
un banco – a bank

Where I Live

Vivo en el centro de la ciudad.	I live in the centre of town.
Vivo en las afueras.	I live in the outskirts.
Vivo cerca de la costa.	I live near the coast.
Mi abuela vive en un pueblo pequeño.	My gran lives in a small village.
Me gustaría vivir en el campo.	I would like to live in the country.

Describing a Town

Mi pueblo es...	My town is...
animado	lively
industrial	industrial
tranquilo	quiet / calm
ruidoso	noisy
concurrido	crowded
limpio	clean
sucio	dirty
bonito	pretty / nice
feo	ugly

aislado	isolated
contaminado	polluted
pintoresco	picturesque

Directions

• **¿Dónde está…?**	Where is…?
• **¿Dónde está el castillo…?**	Where is the castle…?
• **¿Dónde están las tiendas?**	Where are the shops?
• **¿Hay un centro comercial?**	Is there a shopping centre?
• **Sigue todo recto.**	Go straight on.
• **Está a la izquierda.**	It's on the left.
• **Está a la derecha.**	It's on the right.
• **Toma la primera calle.**	Take the first street.
• **Toma la segunda calle.**	Take the second street.
• **Cruza la plaza.**	Cross the square.

Town or Country?

• **Prefiero vivir en el / la… porque…**	I prefer to live in the… because…
• **En la ciudad…**	In the town…
hay mucho que hacer.	there's lots to do.
hay muchas instalaciones deportivas.	there are lots of sports facilities.
el transporte público es fiable.	public transport is reliable.
el ambiente es genial.	the atmosphere is great.
hay mucha gente.	there are a lot of people.
• **En el campo…**	In the countryside…
hay mucha naturaleza.	there's a lot of nature.
es muy tranquilo.	it's very quiet.
hay poca gente.	there are fewer people.
la vida es menos estresante.	life is less stressful.

Key Vocab	
el campo	the country / countryside
hay mucho que hacer	there's lots to do
la ciudad	the city / town
mucha gente	many people

> ## Quick Test
>
> 1. What is the opposite of **ruidoso**, **limpio** and **feo**?
> 2. Translate the following into Spanish: I prefer to live in the town.
> 3. Which is correct: **mucha gente** or **muchas gente** for many people?
> 4. Translate the following into English: **Hay mucho que hacer.**

Where I Live 2

You must be able to:

- Say what there is or isn't where you live
- Talk about what you can or can't do
- Say what improvements you would like to see
- Recognise and name shops.

Saying 'there is / are'

- **hay** — there is / there are
- **En mi pueblo hay un teatro, pero no hay cine.** — In my town there is a theatre but there isn't a cinema.
- **No hay muchas tiendas.** — There are not many shops.
- **Hay muchos turistas.** — There are a lot of tourists.
- **Hay mucha gente.** — There are a lot of people.
- **Hay suficientes parques.** — There are enough parks.
- **No hay suficientes museos.** — There aren't enough museums.

> ### Key Point
>
> Use **mucho / a / os / as** to say 'there is a lot of / many':
> **muchos mercados** – many markets (masc. plural);
> **muchas piscinas** – many pools (fem. plural).
> **Suficiente** does not change for masc. / fem. Just add -s for the plural.

Things to Do

- **se puede / no se puede** — you can / you can't
- **Se puede ir a la playa.** — You can go to the beach.
- **Se puede hacer muchos deportes.** — You can do many sports.
- **Se puede pasear en el parque.** — You can walk in the park.
- **Se puede ir a partidos de fútbol.** — You can go to football matches.
- **No se puede hacer patinaje.** — You can't do skating.
- **No se puede ir al cine.** — You can't go to the cinema.

Improving My Town

- **Me gustaría…** — I would like…
  Me gustaría ver más espacios verdes. — I would like to see more green spaces.
- **Quiero ver menos basura en la calle.** — I want to see less rubbish in the street.
  Quiero ver menos tráfico. — I want to see less traffic.
- **Deben quitar el grafiti.** — They should get rid of the graffiti.
  Deben construir más zonas peatonales. — They should build more pedestrian areas.
  Deben reducir la polución. — They should reduce pollution.

Shops

- Shopping in independent shops is one of the nicest aspects of visiting Spain. Here is a list of shops you will see around most towns:

la panadería	bakery
la zapatería	shoe shop
la papelería	stationery shop
la frutería	greengrocer
la joyería	jeweller
la carnicería	butcher
la pastelería	cake shop
la pescadería	fishmonger
la librería	bookshop
la peluquería	hairdresser
la farmacia	pharmacy

Adding Variety to your Language

- When describing or writing about your town, add in some shops and even what you can buy in them to add some variety. Here are some examples in a range of tenses:

- **Hay una frutería donde se puede comprar uvas, melones y fresas.**
  There is a greengrocer where you can buy grapes, melons and strawberries.
- **Necesito comprar pan fresco en la panadería.**
  I need to buy fresh bread at the bakery.
- **Cuando fui a la joyería compré una pulsera para mi abuela.**
  When I went to the jewellers I bought a bracelet for my gran.
- **Me gustaría comprar un diccionario y el sábado voy a ir a la librería.**
  I would like to buy a dictionary and on Saturday I am going to go to the bookshop.

Quick Test

1. Complete the sentences:
   Puedo ver una película en _____ _____
   Se puede comprar ropa en el _____ _____
   Se _____ comprar fruta en _____ _____
2. Translate the following into Spanish:
   There are many swimming pools.
   There aren't enough parks.
3. Translate the following into English:
   En mi pueblo, me gustaría ver más espacios verdes y menos tráfico.
4. How do you say 'I want' in Spanish?

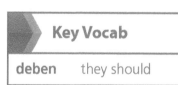

Key Vocab

deben	they should

Holidays 1

You must be able to:

- Name countries and nationalities / languages
- Describe where you usually go on holiday and give some details
- Use prepositions with countries and means of transport.

Countries and Languages

España	**el** español	Spain	Spanish
Inglaterra	**el** inglés	England	English
Francia	**el** francés	France	French
Italia	**el** italiano	Italy	Italian
Alemania	**el** alemán	Germany	German
Polonia	**el** polaco	Poland	Polish
Portugal	**el** portugués	Portugal	Portuguese

> ### Key Point
>
> Most countries don't take an article, e.g. **Voy a Francia** – I go to France. But some do (see*), e.g. **Vamos a los Estados Unidos** – We are going / we go to the United States.

More Countries

los Estados Unidos*	USA
la India*	India
Irlanda (del norte)	(Northern) Ireland
Gales	Wales
Escocia	Scotland
Suiza	Switzerland
Grecia	Greece

Places

la costa	the coast
las montañas	the mountains
el campo	the countryside
el extranjero	abroad

Giving Details

¿Adónde vas de vacaciones?	Where do you go on holiday?
Normalmente voy a…	I usually go to…
¿Con quién vas?	Who do you go with?
Voy con…	I go with…
mis padres / mi familia / mis amigos.	my parents / my family / my friends.
¿Por cuánto tiempo vas?	How long do you go for?
Voy por tres días / dos semanas / un mes.	I go for three days / two weeks / one month.

Means of Transport

el coche	car
el tren	train
el avión	plane
el barco	boat
el autobús	bus
el autocar	coach
la bicicleta	bike
ir en tren	to go by train
Voy en avión.	I go by plane.

Opinions

- **Prefiero ir en barco.** — I prefer to go by boat.
- **No me gusta ir en autocar.** — I don't like going by coach.
- **… porque es más rápido** — … because it's quicker
  … porque no es cómodo — … because it's not comfortable
  … porque es menos caro — … because it's less expensive

Using the Past and Immediate Future

- To talk in the past about your holiday use:

Fui	I went
Fuimos	We went

- To talk in the future use:

Voy a ir	I am going to go
Voy a visitar	I am going to visit
Vamos a hacer	We are going to do
Vamos a nadar.	We are going to swim.

Quick Test

1. Fill in the gaps:
   Voy a Madrid que está en _____
   Hablo _____ en México.
2. Answer in Spanish: **¿Con quién vas de vacaciones?**
3. Finish the sentence: **Prefiero ir en avión porque**
   e_____ m_____ r_____
4. Say in Spanish 'I went to the coast in July.'

Key Vocab

¿Adónde vas de vacaciones?	Where do you go on holiday?
el autocar	coach
el avión	plane
el coche	car
el barco	boat
el tren	train
España	Spain
español	Spanish

Holidays 2

You must be able to:
- Name different types of accommodation
- Talk about holiday activities in the present tense
- Make a reservation.

Accommodation

- **el alojamiento** — accommodation
- **Me quedo en...** — I stay...
- **un hotel de tres, cuatro estrellas** — three-, four-star hotel
- **una tienda de campaña** — a tent
- **una caravana** — a caravan
- **un albergue juvenil** — a youth hostel
- **la casa de mi tía** — my aunt's house

Holiday Activities

- **ir a la playa** — to go to the beach
- **Voy a la piscina.** — I go to the pool.
- **Fui de excursión para visitar los monumentos.** — I went on a trip to visit monuments.
- **Visito los museos.** — I visit museums.
- **Me encanta visitar los sitios de interés.** — I love to visit places of interest.
- **hacer deportes** — to do sports
  Hago vela. — I do / go sailing.
  Hice ciclismo. — I went cycling.
- **sacar fotos** — to take photos
  Saco fotos del pueblo. — I take photos of the town.
- **relajarse** — to relax
  Me gusta relajarme. — I like to relax.
- **ir de compras** — to go shopping
  Voy de compras en las tiendas pequeñas. — I go shopping in the small shops.
  Fuimos de compras en Zara. — We went shopping in Zara.

Key Point

Try to learn the infinitive of the verb rather than just the first-person present tense.

Nadar	to swim
Nado / nadamos	I / we swim
Ir	to go
Voy / vamos	I go / we go
Hacer	to do
Hago / hacemos	I do / we do

As you become more confident you will be able to change the infinitive to the past and future tenses too.

Making a Reservation

- **Me gustaría reservar...**   I would like to book...
  una habitación individual   a single room
  una habitación doble   a double room
  para tres noches   for three nights
  para dos personas   for two people
  con ducha / bañera   with a shower / bath
  con balcón   with a balcony
  con vista al mar   with a sea view
- **¿Cuánto es?**   How much is it?
  ¿Hay wifi?   Is there wi-fi?
  ¿El desayuno está incluido?   Is breakfast included?

Making a Complaint

- **El wifi no funciona.**   The wi-fi isn't working.
- **La luz** no funciona.   The light isn't working.
- **La cama está rota.**   The bed is broken.
- **La ducha** está rota.   The shower isn't working.
- **es ruidoso / sucio**   it's noisy / dirty
- **No hay toallas.**   There are no towels.
- **No hay papel higiénico.**   There's no toilet roll.

The Weather

- **¿Qué tiempo hace?**   What's the weather like?
- Hace sol.   It's sunny.
  Hace buen tiempo.   The weather's good.
  Hace mal tiempo.   The weather's bad.
- Hace calor / frío.   It's hot / cold.
  Llueve / nieva.   It's raining / snowing.
- **Cuando hace sol voy a la playa.**   When it's sunny I go to the beach.

Key Vocab

está roto / a	it's broken
hace sol / calor / frío	it's sunny / hot / cold
Me gustaría reservar...	I would like to reserve...
no funciona	it's not working
para tres noches	for three nights

Quick Test

1. Translate the following into Spanish:
   I relax on the beach with my parents.
2. Ask in Spanish for a double room for one week with a sea view.
3. Ask your friend if he / she likes to take photos.
4. Fill in the gaps: Cuando _____ sol nado en la _____

Global Issues 1

You must be able to:

- Use opinion phrases
- Use adverbs of quantity
- Talk about energy and environmental concerns.

Giving Opinions

- **Creo que**   I believe that
- **Pienso que**   I think that
- **En mi opinión**   In my opinion
- **Encuentro que**   I find that
- **(No) Estoy de acuerdo**   I agree / don't agree
- **Estoy a favor**   I am for
- **Estoy en contra**   I am against
- **Por un lado**   On the one hand
- **Por otro lado**   On the other hand

Adverbs of Quantity

- **mucho / a / os / as**   a lot / many
- tanto / a / os / as   so much / so many
- demasiado / a / os / as   too much / too many
- poco / a / os / as   little / few
- **un poco**   a bit / a little
- **Hay tanto grafiti.** (masc. sing.)   There is so much graffiti.
- **Hay tantos coches.** (masc. plural) There are so many cars.
- Note that **gente**, people, is singular and feminine, i.e. the people is. **Hay demasiada gente.** (fem. sing.) There are too many people.

Dos and Don'ts

- tener que   to have to
- **tienes que**   you have to
- **tenemos que**   we have to
- This is a really useful phrase which you can use for many topics, remember to use the infinitive after it: **Tengo que tomar el autobús.**   I have to take the bus.

Key Point

Muy means 'very' and **mucho** means 'a lot / many'. **Muy** goes before an adjective, e.g. **Mi pueblo es muy histórico** – My town is very historical. **Mucho** goes before a noun, e.g. **Hay muchos monumentos** – There are a lot of / many monuments.

Saving Energy

- You can also use:

debo / se debe / debes (deber)	I should / one should / you should.
Debes…	You should…
apagar las luces cuando no las necesites	turn off the lights when you don't need them
bajar la calefacción	turn down the heating
ir a pie al colegio	walk to school
ir en transporte público	to go by public transport
ahorrar agua	save water
cerrar el grifo cuando te lavas los dientes	turn off the tap when you are brushing your teeth
usar la energía solar	use solar energy
cultivar vegetales y fruta en tu jardín	grow fruit and veg in your garden
donar tu ropa vieja	donate your old clothes.
No debes…	You should not…
malgastar energía	waste energy
malgastar papel	waste paper
usar el coche demasiado	use the car too much
comprar ropa cuando no la necesites	buy clothes when you don't need them

Quick Test

1. How do you say 'I have to' in Spanish?
2. Unravel this sentence:
   Tráfico el hay de demasiado centro en Londres.
   Then translate it into English.
3. How do you say 'I should not waste water' in Spanish?
4. Fill in the gaps with **muy / mucho**:
   Creo que hay _____ ruido en mi pueblo, prefiero vivir en el campo porque es _____ tranquilo.

Key Vocab

demasiado / a / os / as	too much / many
poco / a / os / as	little / few
tanto / a / os / as	so much / many
tener que	to have to

Global Issues 2

You must be able to:

- Say what concerns you
- Talk about global issues
- Talk about ways to address such issues.

Problems and Priorities

- **Lo que me preocupa mucho es…**   What worries me a lot is…
- **Estoy preocupado / a por…**   I am worried about…
- **Me preocupa…**   I am worried about…
- **El mayor problema es…**   The biggest problem is…

Current Issues

- **el desempleo / el paro**   unemployment
  el hambre   hunger
  los refugiados   refugees
  la guerra   war
  la crisis económica   economic crisis
  la gente sin techo   homeless people
  los animales en peligro de extinción   animals in danger of extinction
  la pobreza   poverty
  el trabajo infantil   child labour
  la globalización   globalisation
  el terrorismo   terrorism
  el calentamiento global   global warming
  las inundaciones   flooding
  la crueldad de los animales   animal cruelty
  la contaminación   pollution
  las noticias falsas   fake news
  la deforestación   deforestation

Key Point

Certain adjectives precede the noun instead of following it, for example:

el mayor problema   the biggest problem
una buena comida   a good meal
la próxima clase   the next class
la última vez   the last time

Addressing Problems

• **Es necesario…**	It is necessary…
• **Es importante…**	It is important…
• **Se debe / debemos…**	We must…
• **Todo el mundo** debería…	Everyone should…
ser responsables	be responsible
respetar a los demás	respect others
comprar menos ropa	buy fewer clothes
donar la ropa a la caridad	to donate clothes to charity
proteger a los animales	to protect animals
ayudar a la gente menos afortunada	to help those less fortunate
reciclar en casa	to recycle at home
usar el transporte público	to use public transport
apoyar a las caridades	to support charities
apreciar lo que tenemos	to appreciate what we have
ser menos influenciado / a por las redes sociales	to be less influenced by social media
tomar interés en la política.	to take an interest in politics.

Two-verb and Modal Verb Phrases

Remember that after some verbs the second verb in the sentence must be in the infinitive. Using these two-verb phrases correctly will really improve the quality of your language.

• **Intento ayudar a la gente.**	I try to help people.
• **Quiero comprar menos ropa.**	I want to buy fewer clothes.
• **Es importante ser responsable.**	It is important to be responsible.

The first verb can be in a different tense too, and the same rule applies.

• **Tuve que usar el transporte público.**	I had to use public transport.
• **Me gustó ayudar a mi vecino.**	I liked helping my neighbour.

Key Vocab

debería + infinitive	one / we should + infinitive
el mayor problema	the greatest / biggest problem
estoy preocupado / a por…	I am worried about…
me preocupa…	I am worried about…

Review Questions

Use a separate piece of paper for your answers, if necessary.

School and Education

1 What subject are these people describing? Choose the correct picture.

A    **B**    **C**    **D**

E    **F**    **G**

a) **Estudio fechas importantes como las fechas de batallas.** ....

b) **Escribo poesía y leo las obras de Shakespeare.** ....

c) **Toco la flauta y la guitarra. También canto en el coro.** ....

d) **Hago cálculos.** ....

e) **Trabajo con el ordenador.** .... [5]

2 Choose the answer which fits best.

a) **Me mola el inglés porque es...** ....

    fácil.   **aburrido.**   **chungo.**

b) **No soporto la música porque es...** ....

    inútil.   **súper.**   **genial.**

c) **Me gusta la geografía porque el profe es...** ....

    severo.   **divertido.**   **antipático.**

d) **Odio el inglés porque es...** ....

    útil.   **fácil.**   **aburrido.**   [4]

Future Plans

1 ¿Quién trabaja en...

a) ... un hospital? ....

b) ... una oficina? ....

c) ... una tienda? .... [3]

2 What is wrong with this sentence?

Soy un médico. .... [1]

3 Add the most appropriate time phrase to these statements:

En el futuro	En dos años	En cuatro años

a) .... **voy a ir a la universidad.**

b) .... **voy a dejar el colegio.**

c) .... **voy a casarme.** [3]

4 Complete the sentences with a valid reason why you will or will not study these subjects.
In each case, look at the words in purple for a clue.

a) .... en **inglés pues, lo estudiaré en el colegio mayor.**

b) .... de **español.**

c) **No** .... el **francés.** [3]

5 Fill in the gaps by choosing the correct options from below.

una oficina	diseñador web	dinámico	crear	inspirador

Él es .... **y trabaja en** .... **Le gusta**

mucho su trabajo porque es verdaderamente .... **Puede** ....

nuevos sitios web. Para ser un buen compañero de trabajo es necesario ser

.... [5]

Review Questions

Use a separate piece of paper for your answers, if necessary.

Leisure

1 Add in the correct form of the verb **tocar** for each sentence.

a) _____ el piano pero debo practicar más.

b) Mi hermana _____ muy mal el violín.

c) Me gustaría _____ la flauta pero no tengo tiempo.

d) En el futuro voy a _____ más la guitarra.

e) Mi primo y yo _____ la batería en un grupo de rock. [5]

2 Unjumble these sentences.

a) música me es clásica gusta relajante escuchar porque la.

b) grupo mi americano favorito es.

c) escuchar porque salsa es música la prefiero rítmica.

d) fui concierto ayer de a rock un.

e) ¿gustaría escuchar en te música la vivo? [5

3 Fill in the gaps with **al / a la / a las**.

a) Voy _____ museo de arte porque me interesa mucho.

b) ¿Te gustaría ir _____ tiendas el sábado?

c) Ayer fui _____ club de jóvenes, ¡lo pasé muy bien!

d) ¿Te apetece ir _____ cine el viernes?

e) Normalmente vamos _____ bolera cuando llueve. [5

4 Read the paragraph and fill in the words below in the correct place.

ciencia	sábado	geniales	llamo	son

Hola me _____ Benji y me gustan mucho las películas de

ficción. Creo que _____ emocionantes y los efectos especiales son

_____. Fui al cine el _____ pasado, ¡lo pasé muy bien! [5

TV and Technology

1 For each programme write the genre or category.

a) *I'm a Celebrity Get Me of Here* ....

b) *Our Planet* .... **c)** *EastEnders* ....

d) *The Simpsons* .... **e)** *Match of the Day* ....

f) *The News at Ten* .... [6]

2 Translate these sentences into Spanish.

a) I always watch the news because it is informative.

b) My dad often watches documentaries about history. [about = **sobre**]

c) Do you like to watch soaps?

d) On Sunday I am going to watch a Netflix series with my mum.

e) I prefer to watch cartoons because they are funny and entertaining. [10]

3 Label the parts of the sentence using **a)**–**f)**.

El fin de semana me encanta ver las emisiones de deportes, creo que son muy emocionantes.

a) time phrase **b)** infinitive verb **c)** opinion phrase

d) adjective **e)** intensifier **f)** noun [6]

4 Name in Spanish three things you can do with your mobile phone.

i) ....

ii) ....

iii) .... [3]

5 For each sentence choose the correct form.

mucho	mucha	muchos	muchas

a) Creo que hay .... **ciberacoso en mi colegio.**

b) Hay .... **personas peligrosas en los 'chats'.**

c) Hay .... **que hacer en línea.**

d) Veo .... **violencia en los clips de YouTube.**

e) Es estresante hacer .... **de mis cursos en línea!** [5]

Practice Questions

Use a separate piece of paper for your answers, if necessary.

Shopping and Money

1 Put these words in the correct order.

a) una   llevo   blanca   camisa

b) chaqueta   de   una   negra   llevo   cuero

c) llevar   ropa   prefiero   moda   de

d) vaqueros   al   gustaría   colegio   me   llevar   [4]

2 Change the ending of the colour, if necessary, to match the item of clothing. For example, **Llevo una corbata rojo. – Llevo una corbata roja.**

a) **Me gustan mis botas marrón.**

b) **El fin de semana prefiero llevar mis zapatillas de deporte blanco.**

c) **Ayer compré una sudadera amarillo y gris.**   [3]

3 Complete the shopping dialogue.

Buenos días, ¿en qué puedo servirle?

a) _____ **unos zapatos.**

¿Qué b) _____ **?**

38.

¿Qué c) _____ **prefiere?**

Negro o marrón.

Aquí tiene...

Me gustan estos, d) ¿ _____ **?**

65 euros.

¡Muy bien, los llevo!   [4]

4 Rearrange these words to make a sentence about pocket money.

    Cada   recibo   compro   libras   semana   y   de moda   revistas   cinco   [1]

Where I Live

1 Fill in each gap with the correct place you can do these activities.

a) **Puedo jugar al squash y al tenis de mesa en el** _____.

b) **Voy al** _____ **para comprar ropa y maquillaje.**

c) **Me encanta ir al** _____ **para aprender sobre la historia local.**

d) **Ayer fui al** _____ **y compré manzanas, patatas y cebollas.**

e) **Me gustaría ir al** _____ **para ver un partido de fútbol de mi equipo favorito.**

f) **Hay una** _____ **cerca de mi casa donde leo libros y revistas.** [6]

2 For each statement decide if it relates to the Town (T) or Country (C) and then for each sentence <u>underline</u> the verbs. For example, **<u>Hay</u> mucha gente y siempre <u>está</u> concurrido.**

a) **La vida puede ser estresante.**

b) **Se puede respirar aire limpio.**

c) **Siempre hay mucho que hacer.**

d) **Tengo que esperar mucho tiempo para el autobús.**

e) **Las vistas son increíbles y hay mucha tranquilidad.** [10]

3 Fill in the directions.

a)

_____

_____

b)

_____

_____

c)

_____

_____

d)

_____

_____

e)

_____

_____

f)

_____

_____ [6]

Use a separate piece of paper for your answers, if necessary.

Holidays

1 Fill in the grid.

Country	Language/Nationality
España	a)
b)	alemán
c)	americano
Inglaterra	d)
e)	italiano
Portugal	f)

[6]

2 Look at the questions and then fill in the answers with the correct verb. Next to each sentence write Present (P), Past (PA) or future (F) to indicate the tense.

a) **¿Adónde vas de vacaciones?** Siempre _____ **a Irlanda con mis tíos.**

b) **¿Cuándo vais?** _____ **al principio de agosto.**

c) **¿Qué actividades haces?** _____ **muchos deportes y visito pueblos.**

d) **¿Cómo fuiste a Gales?** _____ **en coche.**

e) **¿Cuánto tiempo te quedaste?** _____ **cinco días.**

f) **¿Adónde vas a ir en Semana Santa?** _____ **a la casa de mis abuelos en Newcastle**

g) **¿Prefieres ir a las montañas o a la playa?** _____ **ir a las montañas.** [14]

3 Translate these sentences into Spanish.

a) I go to France by boat and by car.

b) We go with my grandparents.

c) I usually stay in a youth hostel in Ireland.

d) I went to Spain last year and I visited many places of interest.

e) I went (did) cycling and played football on the beach.

f) I would like to stay in a five-star hotel but it is expensive. [9

Global Issues

1 **a)** What do the verbs below mean?

    i) ayudar _____   **ii)** apoyar _____

    iii) ser _____   **iv) hacer** _____   [4]

    b) Put each verb into the first person – present, preterite (past) and immediate future.   [12]

2 Match up the two halves so they make sense.

Apreciar	el transporte público.
Usar	ropa y comida.
Tomar	lo que tenemos.
Ser	interés en la política.
Donar	responsable.

    [5]

3 Reorder this sentence and then write it in English.

gente a ayudar sin intento techo la.   [2]

4 Fill the gaps with the missing verbs.

voy	donamos	tomo	es	reciclamos	escuchar	uso

Me llamo Silvia y creo que todos deben ser responsables en cuanto a nuestra sociedad. Yo, por

mi parte _____ **mucho interés en la política e intento** _____ **las**

noticias. Además, _____ **el transporte público o** _____ **en bicicleta**

si puedo. Mi madre _____ **miembro de un club ecologista y por eso**

_____ **papel y botellas y** _____ **ropa y comida a las caridades para**

gente menos afortunada.   [7]

5 Correct this sentence and then explain the two errors.

Ayer uso el transporte público y mañana voy a reciclo papel en el colegio.   [2]

Gender and Plurals

You must be able to:

- Use the correct articles for masculine and feminine words
- Make a singular word plural.

The Indefinite Article

- The words for 'a' and 'some' change according to the gender of the noun and whether it is singular or plural.

Singular		Plural	
Masculine	Feminine	Masculine	Feminine
un perro a dog	**una** jirafa a giraffe	**unos** caballos some horses	**unas** arañas some spiders

- The same applies to saying 'the'.

Singular		Plural	
Masculine	Feminine	Masculine	Feminine
el tío the uncle	**la** abuela the grandma	**los** museos the museums	**las** tiendas the shops

Rules and Exceptions

- Nouns ending in **-o** are usually masculine.
  el pelo   hair
  el chico   boy
- Nouns ending in **-a** are usually feminine.
  la playa   beach
  la hermana   sister
- Exceptions to the rule:
  el día (masc.)   day
  el mapa (masc.)   map
  la mano (fem.)   hand
  la foto (fem.)   photo

> ### Key Point
>
> When you learn a new word you should learn the gender.
>
> These rules will help:
>
> Nouns ending in **-ión**, **-ción**, **-dad**, **-tad** are feminine: **la región**, **la información**, **la ciudad** (the town), **la libertad** (freedom).
>
> Nouns ending in **-or**, **-ón**, **-és**, **-ema** are masculine: **el actor**, **el ratón** (mouse), **el estrés** (stress), **el problema**.

Plurals of Nouns

- To make a word plural you add **-s**, and **-es** if the word does not end in a vowel. Don't forget to change the article! (See the table on page 74.)

la chica	the girl
las chicas	the girls
el elefante	the elephant
los elefantes	the elephants

- But:

el profesor	the teacher
los profesores	the teachers
la ciudad	the town
las ciudades	the towns

- Note that words ending in **-z** change the **-z** to a **-c** and add **-es**.

una vez	one time / once
dos veces	twice
un pez	a fish
tres peces	three fish

Uses of the Definite and Indefinite Article

- The definite article is sometimes used in Spanish when we don't use it in English.
- With likes and dislikes:

Me gusta <u>el</u> español.	I like Spanish.
No soporto <u>las</u> telenovelas.	I can't stand soaps.
Prefiero <u>la</u> carne.	I prefer meat.

- With days of the week:

<u>El</u> sábado voy al mercado.	On Saturday I go to the market.
<u>Los</u> martes juego al tenis de mesa.	On Tuesdays I play table tennis.

- Do not use **un / una** when saying what someone does for a job:

Mi madre es enfermera.	My mum is a nurse.
Quiero ser electricista.	I want to be an electrician.

> ## Quick Test
>
> 1. Put the definite articles **(el / la)** in front of these nouns.
>   _____ gato _____ bolera _____ tema _____ ciudad
> 2. Write these words in the plural.
>   el caballo   el profesor   la ciudad   el actor
> 3. Put this sentence into the plural.
>   Hay una goma, un bolígrafo, un lapiz en el estuche.
> 4. How do you say 'the day' in Spanish?

Adjectives

You must be able to:

- Understand the position of an adjective
- Make appropriate changes to an adjective according to the gender of the noun it qualifies
- Use comparatives and superlatives to compare things, people and actions.

Adjectives

- Adjectives are words which describe nouns. In Spanish, adjectives generally come after the noun.
  un conejo blanco   a white rabbit (a rabbit white!)
- In Spanish, adjectives change according to the nouns they describe; singular or plural, masculine or feminine.

Adjectives ending in:	Masculine singular	Feminine singular	Masculine plural	Feminine plural
-o	roj**o** el apartamento modern**o**	roj**a** la casa blanc**a**	roj**os** los edificios antigu**os**	roj**as** las tiendas car**as**
-e only plural change	grand**e** el profesor amabl**e**	grand**e** la abuela trist**e**	grand**es** los documentos important**es**	grand**es** las chicas elegant**es**
consonant plural add **-es**	gris el hombre feliz	gris la asignatura fácil	gris**es** los cursos difíciles	gris**es** las tareas constantes

- Note that adjectives ending in **-or** have different feminine forms, although they end in a consonant, e.g. **trabajador(a)** – hard-working.
- Colours which come from real items should not change at all. For example:

naranja	orange (fruit)
rosa	rose (flower)
violeta	violet (flower)
tres lápices rosa	three pink pencils
un jersey naranja	an orange jumper
unas paredes violeta	mauve / violet walls

> ### Key Point
>
> Using **mucho** (a lot of) and **muy** (very).
>
> **Mucho** goes before a noun and it changes for masc. / fem. / plural, e.g. **mucho ruido** (a lot of noise), **muchas personas** (many / a lot of people).
>
> **Muy** goes before an adjective, e.g. **Aprender verbos es muy útil** (Learning verbs is very useful). **El viaje fue muy largo** (The journey was very long).

Comparatives

- To compare two things, use:

más...que
more...than

Pablo es <u>más</u> abierto <u>que</u> Gloria.
Pablo is <u>more</u> open <u>than</u> Gloria.

menos...que
less...than

Mi prima es <u>menos</u> tranquila <u>que</u> mi hermana.
My cousin is <u>less</u> calm <u>than</u> my sister.

tan...como
as...as

Tocar la flauta es <u>tan</u> difícil <u>como</u> tocar la trompeta.
Playing the flute is <u>as</u> difficult <u>as</u> playing the trumpet.

Superlatives

el / la / los / las... más....
the most...

Señor González es <u>el</u> profesor <u>más</u> gracioso.
Mr González is <u>the</u> funni<u>est</u> teacher.
Juana es <u>la más</u> alta en la clase.
Juana is <u>the</u> tall<u>est</u> in the class.
Los conejos son <u>los más</u> monos.
Rabbits are <u>the</u> cut<u>est</u> (the rabbits are <u>the most</u> cute).

> ### Quick Test
>
> 1. Make these sentences plural.
>   El chico bajo.
>   La asignatura fácil.
>   El bolígrafo naranja.
> 2. **Muy** or **mucho?**
>   **ruido** (noise), **repetitivo, impresionante, turismo**
> 3. Fill in the gaps to compare.
>   Londres es _____ grande _____ Cardiff.
>   El español es _____ difícil _____ el ruso.
>   El helado de chocolate es _____ calorífico
>   _____ el helado de fresa.

tener, ser and estar

You must be able to:

- Understand the uses of **tener**
- Identify when to use **ser and estar**.

tener (to have)

- **tener** is called the infinitive or the title verb. You need to learn the infinitive for all verbs.

tener (to have)

tengo	I have
tienes	you have (sing.)
tiene	he, she, it has
tenemos	we have
tenéis	you have (plural)
tienen	they have

Key Point

To help you remember to use **tener** to express age, why not try singing the following to the tune of 'Happy Birthday':

¿Cuántos años tienes? ×2
¡Tengo...años!
¿Cuãntos años tienes?

Special Uses

tener hambre	to be hungry
No tengo hambre.	I'm not hungry.
tener sed	to be thirsty
¿Tienes sed?	Are you thirsty?

tener	+ age
Tengo trece años.	I am 13 (years old).
Mi tío tiene 40 años.	My uncle is 40 (years old).

tener prisa to be in a hurry
Siempre tengo prisa por la mañana.
I'm always in a hurry in the morning.

tener frío to be cold
Tenemos frío en el invierno.
We are cold in the winter.
tener calor to be hot
Si tengo calor, bebo agua.
If I'm hot, I drink water.

tener ganas de + infinitive   to feel like doing something
No tengo ganas.   I don't feel like it.
No tengo ganas de ir.   I don't feel like going.

ser or estar?

- **ser and estar** both mean 'to be'.

ser (to be)

soy	I am
eres	you are (sing.)
es	he, she, it is
somos	we are
sois	you are (plural)
son	they are

estar (to be)

estoy	I am
estás	you are (sing.)
está	he, she, it is
estamos	we are
estáis	you are (plural)
están	they are

- **ser** is used for:

- More permanent descriptions:
Soy alto.	I am tall.
Es tímida.	She is shy.
- Telling the time:
Es la una.	It's 1 o'clock.
Son las tres.	It's 3 o'clock.
- Jobs:
Es profesor.	He is a teacher.
Soy artista.	I am an artist.

- **estar** is used for:

- Position and location:
  Estoy en Escocia.
  I am in Scotland.
  Estamos en el colegio.
  We are in school.
- Temporary conditions:
  Estoy contento.
  I am happy.
  Mi padre está estresado.
  My dad is stressed.

Quick Test

1. Fill in the correct form of 'tener'.
   Me llamo Fran y _____ el pelo corto.
   Mi profesor de música _____ muchos instrumentos.
   ¿Cuántos años tienes? _____ catorce años.
2. Translate the following sentence into Spanish: I am hungry.
3. ¿es? or ¿está?
   Madrid _____ en España.
   Roma _____ la capital de Italia.
   ¿Dónde _____ ? Estoy en la cocina.
   Mi madre _____ muy enfadada (angry) porque no hice mis deberes.

Regular -ar, -er and -ir Verbs

You must be able to:

* Recognise verbs from the main verb groups
* Start to use **-ar**, **-er**, **-ir** verbs in your sentences.

Main Groups

* There are three main groups of regular verbs in Spanish.

-ar		-er		-ir	
cantar	to sing	**beber**	to drink	**vivir**	to live

-ar Verbs

ayudar (to help)

(yo) ayudo	I help
(tú) ayudas	you help (sing.)
(él, ella) ayuda	he, she helps
(nosotros) ayudamos	we help
(vosotros) ayudáis	you help (plural)
(ellos, ellas) ayudan	they help

* To form present tense of **-ar** verbs:
  1. Start with the infinitive (title of verb) **ayudar**.
  2. Take off the ending, in this case **-ar.**
  3. You have the stem **ayud-**.
  4. Decide which person you are talking about, i.e. I help, she helps, etc.
  5. Look at the table to find the ending, e.g. we **-amos**
  6. Add it on to the stem – **ayudamos** – we help.

* Other regular verbs in this group:

hablar	to talk
viajar	to travel
llegar	to arrive
terminar	to finish / end
llevar	to wear
escuchar	to listen
comprar	to buy
mirar	to watch

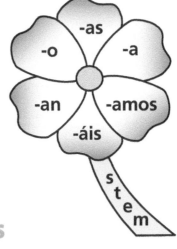

Use of Subject Pronouns

* In Spanish, unlike in English, you can tell which person is being talked about by the verb ending alone.

  Hablo   I speak

  miramos   we watch

* Therefore it is only necessary to use the pronoun if you need to emphasise or when comparing people in a sentence.

> **Key Point**
>
> If a verb is regular, it does not change the stem. But beware! Some verbs are regular in the present tense but irregular in other tenses. You will learn these as you become more familiar with tenses.

Mi madre escucha la música clásica, pero yo escucho la música rap.
My mum listens to classical music but I listen to rap.

-er Verbs

comer (to eat)

(yo) como	I eat
(tú) comes	you eat (sing.)
(él, ella) come	he, she, it eats
(nosotros) comemos	we eat
(vosotros) coméis	you eat (plural)
(ellos, ellas) comen	they eat

-ir Verbs

vivir (to live)

(yo) vivo	I live
(tú) vives	you live (sing.)
(él, ella) vive	he, she, it lives
(nosotros) vivimos	we live
(vosotros) vivís	you live (plural)
(ellos, ellas) viven	they live

- Other regular verbs in this group:

escribir	to write
subir	to go up
imprimir	to print
descubrir	to discover

- The only difference between the **-er** and **-ir** verb endings is the 'we' and 'you' plural.

- Other regular verbs in this group:

aprender	to learn
romper	to break
beber	to drink
creer	to believe
comprender	to understand
coser	to sew
correr	to run
vender	to sell
deber	should

> ### Key Point
>
> It is difficult to learn and apply all six parts of the verb at once. Try and focus on the first person: **hablo** – I speak, and the third person **habla** – he / she speaks. Then, when you are confident with these, go on to the others.

Quick Test

1. Translate these **-ar** verbs into English.
   compro   termina   miramos   ¿escuchas?
2. Now write these in Spanish:
   I arrive   we wear   they look   he listens
3. Write the infinitive of these **-ar / -er / -ir** verbs.
   bebemos   corre   termino   vivís   aprendo
4. Which person do you need for each of these?
   (E.g. **mi amiga** – she or third person.)
   Mis padres   Mi hermano y yo   Mi profesor de inglés

Stem-changing Verbs

You must be able to:

- Understand how the verbs change in each group
- Gradually introduce these tricky verbs into your sentences.

Stem-changing Verbs

- Stem-changing verbs have the same endings as regular verbs but some forms of the verb in the present tense have a vowel change in the stem.
- These verbs are also known as 'boot' verbs because the fourth- and fifth-person verbs ('we' and 'you' plural) keep the original stem.

Group One: e changes to ie

perder (to lose)

pierdo	perdemos
pierdes	perdéis
pierde	pierden

- Other verbs in this group:

pensar	to think
querer	to want, love
empezar	to start
preferir	to prefer
entender	to understand

Group Two: u / o changes to ue

volar (to fly)

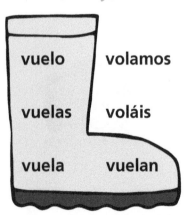

vuelo	volamos
vuelas	voláis
vuela	vuelan

- Other verbs in this group:

jugar	to play
volver	to return
costar	to cost
encontrar	to find
dormir	to sleep
almorzar	to have lunch
poder	to be able

Key Point

These stem-changing verbs are tricky, but you will hopefully already be familiar with some of them, e.g.
Juego al fútbol.
I play football.
llueve   it rains
¿Cuánto cuesta?
How much does it cost?

The more Spanish you learn, the more you will come across them!

Group Three: e changes to i

pedir (to ask for, to order)

pido	pedimos
pides	pedís
pide	piden

- Other verbs in this group to learn:

repetir	to repeat
servir	to serve
vestir(se)	to dress
seguir	to follow

- Stem-changing verbs are usually regular in other tenses.

Duermo ocho horas.	I sleep eight hours.
No dormí anoche.	I didn't sleep last night.
Lo encuentro difícil.	I find it hard.
Encontré tu reloj.	I found your watch.
Prefiero el arroz.	I prefer rice.
Ayer preferí comer patatas.	Yesterday I preferred to eat potatoes.

Quick Test

1. Put these infinitive verbs in the first person present tense.

   jugar   volver   querer   empezar

2. Write this sentence in the 'we' form and then translate it into English.

   Juego al golf si vuelvo temprano del colegio.

3. Translate the following sentence into Spanish:

   When it rains a lot I can't go out and I prefer to watch TV.

hacer, ir and the Immediate Future

You must be able to:

- Understand how to use **hacer** (to do / to make) and **ir** (to go)
- Understand how to form the immediate future.

How to Use hacer

- **Hacer** (to do / to make) is one of the most important verbs to learn. It is known as an irregular verb as the first person has a spelling change.

(yo) hago	I do
(tú) haces	you do (sing.)
(él, ella) hace	he, she, it does
(nosotros) hacemos	we do
(vosotros) hacéis	you do (plural)
(ellos, ellas) hacen	they do

'Hacer' and Weather

In Spanish they say it makes cold / hot / good weather, etc.:

Hace sol – it is sunny.

Hace mal tiempo – it is bad weather.

¿Qué tiempo hace? – what is the weather like?

- One of the most frequent questions you will be asked is:

  ¿Qué haces?   What do you do?

  (**el fin de semana, en el verano, después del colegio**, etc.)

- For example, your teacher may ask:

  ¿Qué haces el fin de semana? What do you do at the weekend?

  To answer this you don't necessarily need to answer with **Hago** (I do). Look at the dialogue:

  A. **¿Qué haces el fin de semana?**

  B. **Voy a la piscina con mis amigos.**

  A **¿Y qué haces después del colegio?**

  B. **Normalmente escucho música o juego al tenis**.

ir (to go)

(yo) voy	I go
(tú) vas	you go (sing.)
(él, ella) va	he, she, it goes
(nosotros) vamos	we go
(vosotros) vais	you go (plural)
(ellos, ellas) van	they go

Key Point

In English we say 'to go' rather than 'to do' for the following examples:

hacer natación
to go swimming

hacer ciclismo
to go cycling

Be aware of this when writing sentences to avoid saying **Voy a la natación, voy al ciclismo.**

The Immediate Future

- You can use **ir + a** followed by the infinitive of any verb to say what you are going to do in the future.

ir – to go	Infinitives	
voy a	hacer	to do
vas a	ir	to go
va a	jugar	to play
vamos a	visitar	to visit
vais a	salir	to go out, leave
van a	cantar	to sing

- **Vamos a visitar a mis abuelos.**   We are going to visit my grandparents.

- **Voy a hacer deporte.**   I am going to do (play) sports.
- **¿Adónde vas a ir?**   Where are you going to go?

- Don't forget, you can extend your sentences (to really impress your teacher!):

  Voy a jugar al baloncesto en el parque con mis primos, ¡será estupendo!
  I am going to play basketball in the park with my cousins, it will be great!
  Voy a salir de mi casa a las diez y después voy a ir al polideportivo.
  I am going to leave home at ten and after that I am going to go to the sports centre.

Negatives and Impersonal Verbs

You must be able to:

- Make sentences negative
- Understand how to use **gustar** and other impersonal verbs correctly.

Making a Sentence Negative

- To make a sentence negative in Spanish is very simple – just put **no** in front of the verb.
  Como legumbres, pero <u>no</u> como carne.
  I eat vegetables but I don't eat meat.
- In longer sentences you will need to put **no** in the right place!
  Fui al mercado ayer, <u>no</u> encontré manzanas pero compré naranjas.
  I went to market yesterday, I didn't find any apples but I bought oranges.
- Sometimes the negatives are in two parts, **no…nunca** and go either side of the verb.
  <u>No</u> veo <u>nunca</u> telenovelas.   I never watch soaps.
  <u>No</u> leo <u>nunca</u> revistas.   I never read magazines.
- Other negative expressions to look out for in reading and listening exercises include:

nadie	no one
ninguno	none
ni…ni	neither…nor

- **Nadie habla el español en mi familia.**
  No one speaks Spanish in my family.
- **Ninguno de mis amigos juega al rugby.**
  None of my friends play rugby.
- **No me gusta ninguno de mis profesores.**
  I don't like any of my teachers.
- **No como ni fruta ni verduras.**
  I eat neither fruit nor vegetables.

Using gustar and Other Impersonal Verbs Correctly

- **Gustar** (to like), is a verb which is very confusing for English speakers; it does not work like the other verbs in Spanish, i.e. you *cannot* say
  Gusto el helado (I like ice cream), you need to say:
  Me gusta el helado.   I like ice cream.
- For plural, say:
  Me gustan los perros.   I like dogs.
- You are in fact saying 'to me I like'.

> **Key Point**
>
> Double negatives don't exist in English but they do in Spanish! 'I don't never do my homework' would be very wrong in English but **No hago nunca mis deberes** is correct in Spanish. 'I don't see nobody' would be equally wrong in English but **No veo a nadie** is correct in Spanish!

- That is why you need to say:
  Me gusta la historia. (sing.)   I like history.
  Me gustan las ciencias. (plural)   I like sciences.

- You can use a verb after **Me gusta** but it must be in the infinitive.
  Me gusta hacer ciclismo.   I like doing (to do) cycling.

- Other verbs which behave like this include:

Me encanta(n)	I love…	**Me encantan las películas de horror.** I love horror films.
Me interesa(n)	I'm interested in…	**Me interesa la geografía.** I'm interested in geography.
Me molesta(n)	… annoy(s) me	**Mi hermano me molesta.** My brother annoys me.
Me duele(n)	… hurt(s) (me)	**Me duelen los pies.** My feet hurt.

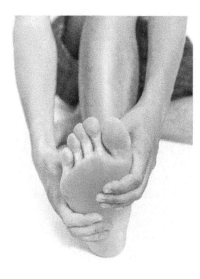

Asking Questions

- To ask a question using these verbs is quite easy:
  ¿Te gusta la comida?   Do you like the food?
  ¿Te gustan los gatos?   Do you like cats?

- Talking about another person:
  Le gusta el pescado.   He / she likes fish.
  No le interesa la lectura.   He / she isn't interested in reading.

Examples: Impersonal Verbs

- Look at this dialogue about school subjects which shows examples of how to use these verbs. See if you can work out what it means.
  A: **Hola Pablo, ¿te gusta aprender el francés?**
  B: **Sí, me gusta el francés pero me interesa más el español porque es más fácil, ¿qué opinas tú Carlota?**
  A: **La verdad es que me molesta el profesor de francés porque es muy estricto, sin embargo me encantan las ciencias y me gusta mucho el profesor de biología porque es gracioso.**
  B: **¡Sí, estoy de acuerdo!**

> ### Quick Test
>
> 1. Translate the following into English: **No veo a nadie en mi casa.**
> 2. Write the sentence in the negative form and then translate it into English: **Siempre bebo zumo por la mañana.**
> 3. In Spanish, ask your friend if she likes dogs.
> 4. Correct the three errors in this sentence:
>   **Me encanta las matemáticas porque es muy fácil.**

Preterite Tense

You must be able to:

- Understand how the preterite is formed for regular verbs
- Use some irregular preterite verbs.

Regular Preterite Verbs

- In Spanish you must use the preterite to talk about what happened in the past. It is used for completed actions, i.e. I bought a T-shirt, or I called my friend.
- These are the verb endings – note that **-er / -ir** verbs take the same endings.

	comprar (to buy)	**aprender** (to learn)	**vivir** (to live)
yo (I)	**compré**	**aprendí**	**viví**
tú (you sing.)	**compraste**	**aprendiste**	**viviste**
él, ella (he, she, it)	**compró**	**aprendió**	**vivió**
nosotros (we)	**compramos**	**aprendimos**	**vivimos**
vosotros (you plural)	**comprasteis**	**aprendisteis**	**vivisteis**
ellos, ellas (they plural)	**compraron**	**aprendieron**	**vivieron**

> **Key Point**
>
> When pronouncing Spanish words the stress naturally falls on the penultimate (second-to-last) vowel; if the word ends in a vowel, **s** or **n**, placing an accent changes this emphasis, e.g. **compró** (stress the **ó**) and **compro** (stress the first **o**).

Irregular Preterite Verbs

- Verbs ending in **-gar** have a spelling change only in the first person.

jugar (to play)

(yo) jugué
(tú) jugaste
(él, ella) jugó
(nosotros) jugamos
(vosotros) jugasteis
(ellos, ellas) jugaron

- Other verbs ending in **-gar**:

llegar	to arrive
entregar	to hand in / submit
pagar	to pay
castigar	to punish

practicar (to practise)

- Verbs ending in **-car** also have a spelling change.

(yo) practiqué
(tú) practicaste
(él, ella) practicó
(nosotros) practicamos
(vosotros) practicasteis
(ellos, ellas) practicaron

- Other verbs ending in **-car**:

tocar	to play an instrument, to touch
sacar	to get, to take out
buscar	to look for

Irregular Preterite Verbs

- These are the most used irregular preterites.

	ser / ir (to be, to go)	hacer (to do, make)	tener (to have)
yo (I)	fui	hice	tuve
tú (you sing.)	fuiste	hiciste	tuviste
él, ella (he, she, it)	fue	hizo	tuvo
nosotros (we)	fuimos	hicimos	tuvimos
vosotros (you plural)	fuisteis	hicisteis	tuvisteis
ellos, ellas (they plural)	fueron	hicieron	tuvieron

Past Tense Time Phrases

Ayer
Yesterday

Anoche
Last night

El sábado pasado
Last Saturday

- Using a time phrase with a verb will always impress!
- **El lunes pasado fui al polideportivo con mis amigos.**
  Last Monday I went to the sports centre with my friends.
- **Anoche hice mis deberes de historia.**
  Last night I did my history homework.

Quick Test

1. Write this present tense sentence in the preterite:
   Hoy voy al parque donde juego al fútbol.
2. Suggest an appropriate time phrase for this sentence, then translate it into English:
   _____ **trabajé con mi madre en el jardín, ¡fue difícil!**
3. Name three **-gar** verbs; what happens in the first person preterite?
4. Translate into Spanish:
   Yesterday I had a Spanish class and I learnt many verbs.

Key Point

Applying the preterite tense accurately to your writing takes time and patience. Start by focusing on the first and third persons and then build up from there.

Use a separate piece of paper for your answers, if necessary.

Shopping and Money

1 Label the clothing the boy is wearing.

[3]

2 Name these materials in English.

a) **algodón** .... b) **cuero** ....

c) **lana** .... [3]

3 Rearrange this sentence and translate it into English.

abrigo   **llevo**   **un**   **y**   **negros**   **unos**   **azul**   **vaqueros**

....

.... [2]

4 You are in a clothes shop in Spain. Speak to the shop assistant.

a) Say you like these brown shoes.

b) Ask if you can try them on.

c) Ask the price. [3]

5 Name **three** chores you do at home.

....

.... [3]

6 Say **two** things you spend your money on. [2]

7 Translate the following sentence into Spanish: Yesterday I worked in the garden.

.... [1]

Where I Live

1 Say where you can do these activities in the town.

a) **Hacer natación.** ....

b) **Comprar ropa.** ....

c) **Ver un partido de fútbol de tu equipo preferido.** ....

d) **Coger un tren.** ....

e) **Ver una película de acción.** .... [5]

2 Fill in each gap with the most appropriate word from the list.

tranquilo	mucho	instalaciones	genial	vida

a) **Hay** .... **que hacer.**

b) **El campo es muy** .... **.**

c) **El ambiente en la ciudad es** .... **.**

d) **La** .... **en el campo es menos estresante.**

e) **Hay muchas** .... **deportivas.** [5]

3 Giving directions in Spain. Match up the two halves of each sentence.

Dónde está el	**cerca.**
Toma la primera calle	**recto.**
Está a cinco minutos	**a la derecha.**
Sigue todo	**a pie.**
Está muy	**castillo.**

[5]

Use a separate piece of paper for your answers, if necessary.

Holidays

1 Fill in the table with the correct countries and nationalities / language.

Country	Nationality
a)	español
b)	inglés
Francia	c)
Alemania	d)
e)	galés
f)	americano

[6]

2 Fill in the correct question phrases.

a) ¿_____ vas de vacaciones? Voy a Irlanda.

b) ¿_____ vas? Voy con mis abuelos.

c) ¿_____ te quedas? Me quedo en una caravana.

d) ¿_____ vas? Voy por dos semanas.

e) ¿_____ vas? Voy en avión.

f) ¿_____ ? Sí, me gusta mucho. [6

3 Look at the details in the table and write what each person says about their holiday.

Person	Place	Who with	How long	Transport	Accommodation	Activity
Simón	Scotland	mum	five days	plane	hotel	eating in restaurants
Javier	mountains	friends	one week	car	youth hostel	hiking
Sara	France	cousin	one month	train	friend's house	practise French

Example: Simón: **Voy a Escocia con mi madre por 5 días. Voy en avión y me quedo en un hotel y como en restaurantes.**

Javier: _____

_____

Sara: _____

_____ [1

4 In Spanish, give two advantages of travelling by plane.

....

.... [2]

5 Translate this past tense question: **¿Adónde fuiste de vacaciones el año pasado?**

.... [1]

Global Issues

1 Fill in the missing words.

a) **La** .... **económica.**   the economic crisis

b) **La** .... **.**   war

c) **Las** .... **.**   floods   [3]

2 Match up the two halves of each sentence.

Es necesario usar	**responsable.**
Es importante reciclar	**a los demás.**
Se debe comprar	**a los menos afortunados.**
Todo el mundo debe ayudar	**papel y botellas en casa.**
Es esencial ser	**menos ropa.**
Es importante respetar	**el transporte público.**

[6]

3 Translate the first two completed sentences in question 2 into English.

a) ....

b) .... [2]

4 Translate into Spanish:

a) I like to help my neighbour.   ....

b) I want to support charities.   ....

c) I am worried about animal cruelty.   .... [3]

Use a separate piece of paper for your answers, if necessary.

Gender, Plurals and Adjectives

1 Fill in the gaps with **el / la / los / las**.

a) .... **chica**   b) .... **profesor**

c) .... **elefante**   d) .... **ciudad**

e) .... **asignaturas**   f) .... **gente**

g) .... **peces**   h) .... **polideportivo**   [8]

2 Put the following phrases into the plural form.

a) **un conejo blanco** ....

b) **una casa azul** ....

c) **una película romántica** ....

d) **la madre estricta** ....

e) **el lápiz rosa** ....

f) **el curso difícil** ....   [6]

3 a) Compare these two people: **Ben es** .... **que** ....   [1]

Ben   Eduardo

b) Fill in the gaps in the sentences below:

Eduardo lleva una camiseta .... **y unos vaqueros**

.... **Ben tiene el pelo** .... **y lleva unos pantalones**

....   [4]

tener, ser, estar and Regular -ar, -er, -ir Verbs

1 Fill in the gap with the correct form of **tener**.

a) Mi padre _____ el pelo gris.

b) Mis primos _____ tres conejos.

c) ¿Tienes hermanos? Sí, _____ una hermana que se llama Leticia.

d) Mi madre y yo _____ los ojos verdes. [4]

2 ¿**estar**? or ¿**ser**? Make sure you change the verb to match the person.

a) Liverpool _____ en Inglaterra.

b) Mi amiga _____ muy inteligente.

c) ¿Dónde estás? _____ en la cocina.

d) En este momento mi padre _____ muy triste.

e) Mis abuelos _____ un poco gordos. [5]

3 Match up these phrases with **tener**.

Tener frío	to be... (years old)
Tener prisa	to feel like
Tener ganas	to be cold
Tener... años	to be thirsty
Tener hambre	to be in a hurry
Tener calor	to be hungry
Tener sed	to be hot

[8]

4 Fill in the correct endings of these present tense verbs.

Me llam_____ Fernando y viv_____ en las afueras de Bogotá que est_____ en Colombia. Mi

hermano y yo nad_____ en la piscina cada sábado, es nuestro deporte favorito. También, yo

practic_____ muchos deportes en el polideportivo. A mi hermano le gusta la música y toc_____

muy bien el piano. Después del colegio yo escuch_____ la radio o jueg_____ videojuegos. Mis

padres v_____ mucho la televisión, les encantan las telenovelas. [9]

Use a separate piece of paper for your answers, if necessary.

Stem-changing Verbs, hacer, ir and the Immediate Future

1 Change these stem-changing verbs to match the person.

a) **Mi colegio** _____ **(empezar) a las ocho y media.**

b) **Yo** _____ **(preferir) los idiomas, pero mi hermana** _____ **(preferir) las ciencias.**

c) **Yo** _____ **(querer) comprar estos zapatos, ¿cuánto** _____ **(costar)?**

d) **Yo** _____ **(jugar) muy bien al rugby, pero mi amigo** _____ **(jugar) bien al fútbol.**

e) **Mis padres y yo** _____ **(poder) ir de vacaciones en agosto.**

f) **No soporto el clima en Inglaterra,** _____ **(llover) demasiado.**   [9]

2 Answer the question below with the most suitable response.

¿Qué haces el fin de semana?

a) **Voy a la natación.**   b) **Hace mucho frío.**

c) **Practico deportes.**   d) **Hice mis deberes.**   [1

3 Translate the following sentence into English:

Voy a ir al cine el domingo próximo, ¡será estupendo!

_____   [2

4 Look at the table and write sentences to describe Pedro and Marcela's plans for the future.

Person	When	Activity	Who with	Opinion
Ignacio	El martes próximo	hacer ciclismo	Hector	competitivo
Pedro	En dos días	viajar a Escocia	mis tíos	emocionante
Marcela	En agosto	hacer un curso de inglés	sola	difícil, divertido

Example: **Ignacio: El martes próximo voy a hacer ciclismo con Hector, será competitivo.**

a) **Pedro**

_____

b) **Marcela**

_____   [8

Negatives, Impersonal Verbs and Preterite Tense

1 Make these sentences negative:

a) **Siempre veo la televisión** _____.

b) **Como carne y pescado** _____.

c) **Todos hablan francés en mi familia** _____. [3]

2 Translate these sentences into Spanish:

a) I love Spanish! _____

b) I like dogs. _____

c) Do you like cats? _____

d) My sister is interested in art. _____

e) My head hurts. _____

f) What do you like to do on Saturdays? _____ [6]

3 Write this sentence in the past tense.

Normalmente voy a la playa en julio, tomo el sol y juego al voleibol, después, compro un helado y bebo una limonada.

_____

_____ [5]

4 Fill in the gaps with the verbs in the preterite, and with the correct person.

Anoche _____ **(ir) al cine con Raúl y** _____ **(ver) una película de ciencia ficción, creo que** _____

(ser) un poco monótona pero me gustó en general. Hoy por la mañana _____ **(tener) una clase**

de historia con Señor Martín, desafortunadamente no _____ **(entregar) mis deberes porque**

no _____ **(tener) tiempo de hacerlos el domingo. En el recreo** _____ **(jugar) al tenis**

de mesa y por eso _____ **(llegar) tarde a mi clase de inglés, ¡qué mal alumno soy!** [8]

Future Tense

You must be able to:

- Understand the difference between the immediate future tense and the simple future tense
- Use both regular and irregular verbs in the future tense
- Use the appropriate time phrase.

The Immediate Future Tense

- We have already looked at the **immediate future tense**. This tense describes what is **going to happen**.

Voy a ir al museo.	I am going to go to the museum.
Vamos a comer en la casa de mi abuela.	We are going to eat at my grandmother's house.

The Simple Future Tense

- This describes what **will happen** in the future.
- To form the future tense you will need the **infinitive** (title verb).
- Add these endings to the infinitive:

yo (I)	**jugaré**	I will play
tú (you sing.)	**jugarás**	you will play
él, ella (he, she, it)	**jugará**	he / she / it will play
nosotros (we)	**jugaremos**	we will play
vosotros (you plural)	**jugaréis**	you will play
ellos, ellas (they plural)	**jugarán**	they will play

- The following have irregular stems in the future, so you will need to add the above endings to the stem:

decir	to say	**diré**	I will say
hacer	to do	**haré**	I will do
poder	to be able	**podré**	I will be able
poner	to put	**pondré**	I will put
querer	to want, to love	**querré**	I will want
saber	to know	**sabré**	I will know
tener	to have	**tendré**	I will have
venir	to come	**vendré**	I will come

- It is fairly flexible regarding which future to use.

Voy a jugar.	I am going to play.
Jugaré.	I will play.

- Either used correctly with a time phrase will improve the quality of your writing.

> ### Key Point
>
> It is important to stress the accented vowel in these verbs; practise saying them out loud, e.g.
> **jugaré** – 'jugareh'
> **tendré** – 'tendreh'

Time Phrases

- It is important to use the correct time phrase with your verbs.
  Using a time phrase can signal to the reader or listener that you are
  changing tense.

Preterite	Present	Future
ayer – yesterday	**hoy** – today	**en el futuro** – in the future
anoche – last night	**normalmente** – usually	**mañana** – tomorrow
hace tres días – three days ago	**ahora** – now	**el año que viene** – the coming year
hace una semana – one week ago	**en este momento** – at this moment	**en un mes** – in one month
el sábado pasado – last Saturday	**hoy en día** – nowadays	**el próximo domingo** – next Sunday
el lunes pasado – last Monday	**actualmente** – currently	**la próxima semana** – next week
el año pasado – last year		

- Examples:
  En una hora voy a comer.
  I am going to eat in one hour.
  Hace dos años fui a Grecia.
  Two years ago I went to Greece.
  Hoy tengo una clase de historia.
  Today I have a history class.
  Normalmente llevo vaqueras pero ayer llevé un vestido.
  I usually wear jeans but yesterday I wore a dress.
- The position of the time phrase can be at the beginning or the end of
  the sentence.

Quick Test

1. Translate the following sentence into English:
   Comeré menos azúcar en el futuro.
2. Put these irregular verbs in the first person future tense:
   hacer   tener   poder   decir
3. Decide which time phrase you could use to improve these
   sentences:
   a) **Voy a ir al centro comercial.**
   b) **Hice ciclismo en el parque.**
   c) **Tengo muchos deberes.**

Pronouns and Reflexive Verbs

You must be able to:

- Use the correct pronoun
- Place the pronoun in the correct position
- Understand how reflexive verbs work.

What is a Pronoun?

- **Subject pronouns** are used less in Spanish because the verb ending usually tells you who is doing the action, i.e. **Com<u>emos</u> chocolate.** We eat chocolate.

- **Object pronouns** replace something or someone that has already been mentioned, e.g. Do you watch **cartoons**? Yes, I watch **them**.

me	**me**
you (sing.)	**te**
him, her, it	**lo, la**
us	**nos**
you (plural)	**os**
them	**los, las**

- Examples:

  La visito.
  I am visiting her.
  Te veo.
  I see you.
- Note: object pronouns usually go <u>before</u> the verb!
- Use an object pronoun to improve your sentences, e.g.

  Siempre compro fruta, compro fruta en el mercado.
  I always buy fruit, I buy fruit at the market.
  Siempre compro fruta, la compro en el mercado.
  I always buy fruit, I buy it at the market.
- In the first sentence, **fruta** is repeated and it sounds a bit clumsy. In the second sentence, the word **fruta** is replaced by its pronoun **la**.
- Object pronouns can be used with any tense, e.g.

  Anoche hice mis deberes**, los hice rápidamente.**
  Last night I did my homework, I did it quickly.
  El viernes voy a cenar pescado**, lo voy a comer con ensalada.**
  On Friday I am going to eat fish, I am going to eat it with salad.

Reflexive Verbs

- Reflexive verbs describe an action which you do to yourself. They always have a special reflexive pronoun to show this.

  Me ducho.   I shower 'myself'.
- In English we do not include 'myself' but in Spanish you must include the pronoun 'me'.
- Some verbs are reflexive and it is not clear why.

  Me llamo…   I am called… (literally 'I call myself')
- In the table below, the first verb **ducharse** is regular and reflexive.
- The second verb **divertirse** is a stem-changing (boot) verb.

	ducharse (to shower)	divertirse (to enjoy oneself)
yo	me ducho	me divierto
tú	te duchas	te diviertes
él, ella	se ducha	se divierte
nosotros / as	nos duchamos	nos divertimos
vosotros / as	os ducháis	os divertís
ellos, ellas	se duchan	se divierten

- When you first start learning reflexive verbs there is a tendency to make all verbs reflexive This should be avoided as it can cause some very strange concepts!

  Me como.   I eat myself!

  Me detesto.   I hate myself!

Useful reflexive verbs	
levantarse	to get up
llevarse con	to get on with a person
despertarse	to wake up
bañarse	to have a bath
acostarse	to go to bed

Quick Test

1. What is an object pronoun and where is it positioned in the sentence?
2. Translate the following into English:

   Los como   ¿Me visitas?   Lo compro   ¿Los hiciste?
3. Translate the following into English: **Me divierto mucho.**
4. Put these infinitive reflexive verbs into the first person and translate them into English.

   llamarse   levantarse   despertarse (this has the same stem change as **divertirse**!)

Imperfect Tense

You must be able to:

- Understand how to use the imperfect tense
- Understand the difference between the preterite and the imperfect.

The Imperfect Tense vs Preterite

- Both tenses are past tenses.
- The preterite tense describes a completed action in the past, i.e. Yesterday I went to the park.
- The imperfect describes:
  - repeated actions in the past
  - what someone was like in the past
  - what things used to be like.
- To form the imperfect tense, add these endings to the stem.

	ar **verbs – add** -aba	er **and** ir **verbs – add** -ía
yo (I)	jug**aba**	viv**ía**
tú (you sing.)	jug**abas**	viv**ías**
él, ella (he, she, it)	jug**aba**	viv**ía**
nosotros (we)	jug**ábamos**	viv**íamos**
vosotros (you plural)	jug**abais**	viv**íais**
ellos, ellas (they plural)	jug**aban**	viv**ían**

- There are only three irregular verbs in the imperfect tense:

ir	(to go)	**iba, ibas, íbamos, ibais, iban**
ser	(to be)	**era, eras, era, éramos, erais, eran**
ver	(to see)	**veía, veías, veía, veíamos, veíais, veían**

Time Phrases and the Imperfect

- Always try and use a time phrase to signal a change of tense.

Anteriormente
Previously

Cada día
Every day

Antes
Before, in the past

En el pasado
In the past

- **Antes jugaba al tenis.**
- **Anteriormente iba de vacaciones a Gales.**

In the past I used to play tennis.
I used to go to Wales on holiday.

hay in the Imperfect

- The imperfect of **hay** (there is) is **había** (there was).
  En el hotel había **una piscina cubierta.**
  In the hotel there was an indoor pool.
  Había **mucha gente en el centro comercial.**
  There were a lot of people in the shopping centre.

Using the Imperfect with a Second Tense

- To improve the quality of your writing and speaking use the present and imperfect in one sentence.
  En el pasado viajaba **en tren pero ahora** voy **en autobús.**
  In the past I used to travel by train but now I go by bus.
  Cuando tenía 12 años tocaba **el piano, pero ahora** toco **la guitarra.**
  When I was 12 I used to play the piano, but now I play the guitar.
- Similarly, using a preterite and imperfect together correctly will impress.
  Cada verano iba **al extranjero pero el año pasado** me quedé **en Inglaterra.**
  Every summer I used to go abroad, but last year I stayed in England.

Describing Someone You Used to See

- Use the imperfect to talk about someone you no longer see.
  Mi abuela era **amable y** tenía **los ojos azules.**
  My gran was nice and she had blue eyes.
  Mi profesor de primaria era **muy paciente y me** ayudaba **mucho.**
  My primary teacher was very patient and he helped me a lot.

Quick Test

1. Put these verbs into the imperfect:
   hablar   ver   vivir   ser
2. Name three time phrases to be used with the imperfect.
3. Translate the following into Spanish:
   I used to go to the park but now I go to the stadium.
4. What does this question mean?
   ¿Cómo eras cuando tenías 10 años?

Conditional Tense and deber

You must be able to:

- Use the conditional tense to say what would happen
- Use **deber** to say what you should do.

Conditional Tense

- The conditional tense is used to express 'would'.
- Use the same stem as the future tense, the endings are the same for **-ar / -er / -ir** verbs.

	ser (to be)
yo (I)	sería
tú (you sing.)	serías
él, ella (he, she, it)	sería
nosotros (we)	seríamos
vosotros (you plural)	seríais
ellos, ellas (they plural)	serían

- The verbs which have irregular stems in the future have the same irregular stems in the conditional.

hacer	to do
haré	I will do
haría	I would do

tener	to have
tendré	I will have
tendría	I would have

salir	to go out / leave
saldré	I will go out
saldría	I would go out

decir	to say
diré	I will say
diría	I would say

poder	to be able
podré	I will be able
podría	I would be able

venir	to come
vendré	I will come
vendría	I would come

Key Point

Me gustaría + infinitive is a useful conditional verb to know.
Me gustaría hacer vela, sería emocionante.
I would like to go sailing, it would be exciting.
¿Te gustaría...?
Would you like to...?

Examples of Conditional Questions and Answers

- **¿Qué te gustaría hacer en el verano?**
  What would you like to do in the summer?
- **Me gustaría ir a la playa, ¡sería estupendo!**
  I would like to go to the beach, it would be great!
- **¿Qué deporte harías?**
  What sport would you do?
- **Jugaría al baloncesto, creo que sería competitivo.**
  I would play basketball, I think it would be competitive.
- **¿Cómo sería tu casa ideal?**
  What would your ideal house be like?
- **Tendría un gimnasio y un jardín enorme.**
  It would have a gym and an enormous garden.

deber (should)

- **Deber** is a very useful verb to express the idea of 'should'; it actually means 'duty', and that is where the word **deberes** comes from, as it is considered a duty to do your homework!
- The verb following it must take the infinitive.
Debo trabajar duro.	I should work hard.
Debemos ayudar en casa.	We should help at home.
- **Se debe** — one should / you should
Se debe reciclar botellas.	You should recycle bottles.
Se debe respetar a los demás.	You should respect others.
- **Debería** is the conditional form and it is still translated as 'should'.
  Debería pasar más tiempo con mis abuelos.
  I should spend more time with my grandparents.

> ### Quick Test
>
> 1. Put these verbs in the first-person conditional:
>   hablar   vivir   tener   hacer
> 2. Translate this question into English:
>   ¿Te gustaría vivir en España en el futuro?
> 3. Put this sentence in the correct order to mean 'You mustn't chew gum in class'.: **en   comer   debe   no   chicle   se   clase**
> 4. Translate the following sentence into Spanish:
>   I should arrive at 9 o'clock.

Use a separate piece of paper for your answers, if necessary.

Future Tense, Pronouns and Reflexive Verbs

1　Put these verbs in the first-person immediate future and then translate them into English.

hablar ....

jugar ....

hacer ....

tener ....　[4]

2　Name three future time phrases.

....　[3]

3　Rewrite these sentences replacing the noun with an object pronoun.

a) **Compro el queso.** ....

b) **Mi madre visita a mis abuelos.** ....　[2]

4　Translate the following into English:

¿Hiciste tus deberes? Sí, los hice hace una hora.

....　[2]

5　Write these reflexive verbs in the present tense 'I' and 'we' form.

　　　　levantarse　　　　**llamarse**　　　　**divertirse**

....

....

....　[6]

6　Translate the following into Spanish:

My friend is called Petra and she will study in Spain next year.

....

....　[3]

Imperfect Tense, Conditional Tense and deber

1 Which tense would you use to translate these questions to Spanish?

I lived in Paris last year. ....

I often practised my French. ....

I went to French classes regularly. ....

I met my boyfriend there. .... [4]

2 Write these verbs in the first person imperfect and add in a time phrase.

Ir a la playa   **trabajar en una tienda**   **hacer muchos deportes**

....

....

.... [6]

3 Use the words in the box below to translate the following sentence into Spanish:

I used to do dance classes and I really liked them.

| antes | clases | hacía | baile | gustaban | de | mucho | me | y |

.... [1]

4 Translate **Me gustaría** into English. .... [1]

5 Write in Spanish:

My ideal house would have a pool and would be modern.

.... [2]

6 Write in Spanish three things you should do or should not do to be a good pupil. For example,
Debería participar bien.
I should participate well.

....

....

.... [3]

Use a separate piece of paper for your answers, if necessary.

Gender, Plurals and Adjectives

1 Write the definite and indefinite form of each of these nouns. Check to see if the noun is singular or plural! For example, **amigo – el amigo**, **un amigo.**

a) Biblioteca ....

b) Centro comercial ....

c) Casas ....

d) Profesores ....

e) Abrigo ....

f) Botas .... [6]

2 Write in Spanish.

a) red shoes ....

b) a blue car ....

c) a black and white jacket ....

d) expensive shops ....

e) brown leather boots ....

f) an orange woollen jumper .... [6

3 Look at the information on these two cities and write sentences to compare them. Use **más / menos** in your answers. For example,

En Bilbao hace más calor que en Glasgow.

In Bilbao it is hotter than in Glasgow.

En el año 2020	Glasgow (Escocia)	Bilbao (España)
Habitantes	599 millones	346 milliones
Número do museos	20	11
La temperatura máxima	25 grados	30 grados
Número de turistas	16 millones	2 millones

a) ....

b) ....

c) .... [

tener, ser, estar, and Regular -ar, -er, -ir Verbs

1 Match up the two halves of each sentence.

Mi abuelo tiene	Trece.
Tengo el pelo	en España.
Madrid está	barba.
¿Cómo eres?	Es muy estricto.
¿Cómo es tu profesor?	Soy muy paciente.
¿Cuántos años tienes?	largo y rizado.

[6]

2 Look at the table and write sentences to describe Lotti, Juanita and Pépe.

Example: **Lotti es alta y tiene los ojos azules, es tímida, tiene dieciocho años y su cumpleaños es el tres de julio.**

	Physical	Character	Age	Birthday
Lotti	alta, ojos azules	tímida	18	tres de julio
Juanita	baja, pelo rizado	amable	12	19 de noviembre
Pépe	pelo rubio, gafas	competitivo	15	25 de enero

a) Juanita ....

b) Pépe .... [10]

3 Underline the verb in each sentence and then translate them into English.

a) Mi madre trabaja en una farmacia cada día. ....

b) Mis abuelos viven en el campo en el norte de Inglaterra. ....

c) Toco el piano después del insti. ....

d) Mi prima y yo nadamos en el mar en el verano. .... [4]

Review Questions

Use a separate piece of paper for your answers, if necessary.

Stem-changing Verbs, hacer, ir and the Immediate Future

1 Fill in the gap with the correct form of the verb in brackets.

a) **(Yo)** _____ **el insti a las ocho y media (empezar).**

b) **Mi tío** _____ **que Liverpool es el mejor equipo (pensar).**

c) **¿Cuánto** _____ **el billete de tren? (costar).**

d) **Mis amigos** _____ **al rugby pero yo** _____ **al fútbol (jugar).**

e) **Desafortunadamente** _____ **mucho en Irlanda (llover).**   [6]

2 Translate the following into English:

a) **¿Qué tiempo hace?** ....

b) **Hace mucho frío.** ....

c) **¿Qué haces después del colegio?** ....

d) **Siempre hago mis deberes.** ....

e) **Hago equitación el sábado.** ....   [5]

3 Correct the error in each of these Spanish translations.

a) My school starts at 8.   **Mi colegio empeza as las 8.**

b) It is cold.   **Es frío.**

c) We play golf on Sunday.   **Juegamos al golf el domingo.**

d) I do lots of sports.   **Haco muchos deportes.**

e) We think it is great.   **Piensamos que es genial.**

f) I return home at 5.   **Volvo a casa a las 5.**   [6]

4 Fill in the gaps to make these future sentences.

a) **Voy a** _____ **a Nueva York en dos años.**

b) **Mis padres** _____ **a comprar una nueva casa el año que viene.**

c) **¿Qué vas a hacer mañana?** _____ **a hacer ciclismo.**

d) **Eduardo** _____ **a trabajar en una granja en el verano.**

e) **Vamos a** _____ **una película sobre la guerra.**   [5]

Negatives, Impersonal Verbs and Preterite Tense

1 Translate these negative sentences.

    a) **Nunca voy al supermercado.**   **b)** **No veo a nadie en el parque.**

    c) **No hago deportes acuáticos.**   **d)** **No hice nada ayer.**   [4]

2 Find the error in each sentence.

    a) **Me gusta los programas de música.** (I like music programmes.)

    b) **A mi padre se gusta la pesca.** (My dad likes fishing.)

    c) **Me encanto la moda.** (I love fashion.)

    d) **Mi profesor de latín me molesto mucho.** (My Latin teacher annoys me a lot.)

    e) **Me duelen el estómago.** (My tummy hurts.)

    f) **¿Te gusta el arte? Sí, te gusta mucho.** (Do you like art? Yes I like it a lot.)   [6]

3 Write the most suitable answer for each question using the prompt.

    Example: **¿Qué compraste ayer? Compré un abrigo.**

    a) **¿Qué comiste anoche?** _____ **pescado y verduras.**

    b) **¿Qué deporte jugaste?** _____ **al hockey sobre hielo.**

    c) **¿Tocaste la guitarra hoy?** _____ **a las dos.**   [3]

4 Write the missing preterite verbs.

    a) **¿Cuánto** _____ **tus zapatos? 50 euros.**

    b) **¿** _____ **miedo? Sí, la película fue espantosa.**

    c) **El fin de semana pasado** _____ **mucho calor.**

    d) **Hace dos horas** _____ **al dentista, ¡fue horrible!**   [4]

Review Questions

Use a separate piece of paper for your answers, if necessary.

Future Tense, Pronouns and Reflexive Verbs

1 Fill in the gaps with the required simple future tense verbs. Use the first person throughout, except for the last one.

El año que viene _____ **(ir) a la universidad para estudiar la historia.**

_____ **en octubre (empezar) y** _____ **(tener) que vivir en un piso**

compartido con tres estudiantes. Creo que _____ **(hacer) muchas actividades**

interesantes y _____ **(ser) estupendo.** [5]

2 Look at the dialogue in a clothes shop and put in pronouns where you think they would fit. Remember the two possible positions for subject pronouns with infinitives! For example:

Quiero escuchar la música – la quiero escuchar *or* **quiero escucharla**

Hola, ¿qué desea?

Quiero comprar unos pantalones.

¿De qué color?

Quiero los pantalones en gris.

No tengo los pantalones en gris, sino en negro y azul marino.

Vale, me gustan estos en negro, ¿puedo probar los pantalones?

Sí, el probador está enfrente…

5 minutos más tarde…

¡Me quedan muy bien! Quiero llevar los pantalones.

¿Algo más?

Sí, necesito un cinturón marrón.

Aquí tiene un cinturón en marrón.

Llevo el cinturón también.

Vale, son 47 euros en total… [5

3 Look at the text and write an **R** next to all the verbs which are reflexive verbs in Spanish.

I am called Sara and here is my daily routine: I wake up at 7 am and I get up 5 minutes later. I have a shower and then I get dressed. I have breakfast at 8 am and then I leave the house. I walk to school and I arrive at school at 8.50 am. I have fun at school because I have many friends there. I always go to bed at 9.30 pm on a school night.

Translate the reflexive verbs into Spanish.

_____

_____   [7]

Imperfect Tense, Conditional Tense and deber

1 Write these sentences using both the present and imperfect tenses. The infinitive verb has been given.

a) I used to drink juice but now I drink water. **(beber)**

_____

b) I used to learn German but now I learn French. **(aprender)**

_____   [2]

2 Which tense(s) would you use to write these sentences in Spanish? Present **PR**, conditional **C**, imperfect **I** or Preterite **P**?

a) I would go to the concert but I don't have enough money.   ....

b) I travelled to Dublin last year with my aunt.   ....

c) Last summer I played tennis every day.   ....

d) I visited many places when I was in Mexico.   ....   [4]

3 Write these verbs – some are regular and some are irregular – in the first person conditional tense, then write what they mean.

a) hacer   ....

b) viajar   ....

c) salir   ....   [3]

Use a separate piece of paper for your answers, if necessary.

1 Write the Spanish for these phrases.

a) I can ....

b) you can ....

c) I can do ....

d) I can visit ....

e) there is ....

f) there was ....

g) there are people ....

h) there was pollution ....

8 marks

2 Put these items into the plural form with the definite articles, e.g. **un museo – los museos**.

a) **un gato** ....

b) **un lápiz** ....

c) **un centro comercial** ....

d) **una catedral** ....

e) **un pez** ....

f) **un profesor de ciencias** ....

6 marks

3 Read what the three people say about themselves, then answer the questions.

¡Hola! Me llamo Antonia y vivo en el sur de España con mi madre porque mis padres están divorciados. Tengo dos hermanastros que son menores que yo. Mi padre vive en el este de España. Normalmente visito a mi padre durante las vacaciones. Adoro los animales y hago equitación dos veces a la semana. Es genial. ¿Y tú, te gustan los animales?

¿Qué tal? Mi nombre es Enrique y vivo en Italia, pero nací en Inglaterra. Vivo con mis padres, pero mi padre trabaja en Inglaterra y viaja mucho. Soy hijo único, pero me gustaría tener una hermana. Me encanta la música y toco el piano y quisiera aprender a tocar la guitarra. ¿Y tú, te gusta la música?

¡Buenos días! Me llamo Laura y vivo en Francia. Tengo trece años y mi cumpleaños es el diecinueve de junio. Mi hermana tiene diez años. Ella es muy amable. Me mola la música pop, pero detesto el rap. Toco la guitarra. ¿Y tú, tocas la guitarra?

a) Who has a sister? ....

b) Who doesn't live with their dad? ....

c) Who loves horses? ....

d) Who plays the guitar? ....

e) Who has a younger sister? ....

5 marks

4 Look at this dialogue about arranging to go out. Translate the English parts into Spanish. Translate 'going' as 'to go'!

Hola Gemma, ¿te apetece salir mañana?

a) Hi, I can't tomorrow but I can on Sunday.

....

Muy bien, hay una nueva película de Disney, ¿te apetece verla?

b) I would love to! What time?

....

Empieza a las dos y media en el Cine Capitol

c) Perfect! Do you fancy going to the pizzeria after the film?

....

4 marks

¡Sí!, ¡qué buena idea! ¡Hasta mañana!

5 Read the text and decide if the sentences are **true** or **false**. Circle each correct answer.

¡Hola! Me llamo Jess y nací el once de diciembre. Tengo catorce años. Tengo un hermano y una hermana. Mi hermana tiene diez años y mi hermano tiene dieciséis años. Vivo con mis padres y mis hermanos en el noroeste de Inglaterra. Me gusta vivir en mi casa porque es bastante grande y porque no tengo que compartir mi dormitorio, sin embargo no me gusta mucho vivir en el norte de Inglaterra porque siempre hace frío. En mi tiempo libre me mola ir a la pista de patinaje con mis amigos. Toco la flauta pero mis hermanos tocan el piano.

a) Jess was born in winter. T / F **b)** Jess is the oldest in the family. T / F

c) There are five people in her family. T / F **d)** Jess likes her house. T / F

e) Jess shares her bedroom. T / F **f)** Jess plays the piano and the flute. T / F

6 marks

6 Match the two halves of these sentences.

Mi pueblo es muy animado y	y tranquilo.
Mi pueblo es muy aislado	en el jardín botánico.
El aire está muy contaminado	estupendas.
Hay muchas flores y árboles	a causa de los atascos.
Hay demasiada gente y	tiendas.
No hay suficientes	hay mucho que hacer.
Hay un mercado donde se puede	está concurrido.
Las instalaciones deportivas son	comprar fruta y verduras.

8 marks

7 Read what these people say about food and drink, then answer the questions.

Jaime:

Me chifla el filete con patatas fritas pero la paella es mi plato favorito, sobre todo la paella de mariscos. Me encanta el pescado. Aunque detesto los postres, prefiero el queso. Desayuno mucho café y tortilla española.

Marisa:

Detesto el pescado y los mariscos. Como queso rara vez y nunca como pizza. Me gustan mucho las berenjenas, las zanahorias y los guisantes. Todos los días desayuno un chocolate caliente con churros.

Selina:

Me encantan los espaguetis y las pizzas. No soporto los huevos porque para mí el sabor es repugnante. Me gusta beber una botella de agua mineral porque es buena para la salud.

a) Who prefers a cold drink?

b) Who likes vegetables?

c) Who does not like eating sweet things?

d) Who likes Italian food?

e) Who would not eat an omelette?

f) Who does not like fish?

6 marks

8 Fill in the gaps with the verbs in the present tense.

Soy Ramón y a) _____ (tener) un trabajo a tiempo parcial en una tienda de ropa.

b) _____ (empezar) a las 9 y termino a las 5. Me gusta mucho el trabajo

porque mis compañeras de trabajo c) _____ (ser) ambles y me ayudan mucho.

d) _____ (ganar) 45 euros al día, no es mucho, pero puedo e) _____

(comprar) videojuegos y ropa con el dinero.

5 marks

9 Match up the two halves of the sentences below.

No voy a hablar;	me duele la mano.
Voy a ir al dentista;	me duele la cabeza.
Quiero unas aspirinas;	me duelen los pies.
No puedo comer;	tengo dolor de garganta.
No puedo hacer mis deberes;	me duelen los dientes.
No quiero ir de paseo;	tengo dolor de estómago.

6 marks

10 Read this letter of complaint written to a hotel and answer the questions in English.

Muy señor mío,

Le escribo para quejarme de mi estancia en su hotel al final de junio este año. Reservamos una habitación con dos camas y ducha, pero cuando llegamos no había agua caliente y la habitación era muy pequeña. Además, la vista desde nuestra habitación era del aparcamiento y era muy fea. El ascensor no funcionaba y fue un problema porque mi padre tiene 78 años y nuestra habitación estaba en la quinta planta. No estoy nada contenta y quiero un reembolso del 50%.

Atentamente,
Marisol Amaya

a) When did Marisol stay at the hotel?

_____

b) What were the first two issues she had?

_____

c) Why was the broken lift particularly an issue?

_____

d) What outcome does she want?

_____

☐

4 marks

11 Translate the English parts of this dialogue about booking a hotel.

Buenos días, ¿Qué desea?

a) I would like to book a double room for July.

_____

Sí, claro, ¿para qué fechas?

b) 3–11 July

_____

¿Para cuántas personas?

c) For three people, two adults and a child.

_____

Muy bien, tenemos una habitación con balcón para estas fechas.

d) How much is it?

_____

Son 400 euros.

e) Is breakfast included?

_____

Sí, está incluido.

f) Perfect!

_____

☐

6 marks

12 Rearrange the following words to create a sentence about jobs.

| otros | trabajo | me | médico | gusta | ayudar | a | porque | como |

☐

5 marks

_____

13 Put these phrases into order by numbering them 1–5, with 1 being what you would do first.

a) **Voy al instituto.**

b) **Voy a aprobar mis exámenes de GCSE.**

c) **Voy a dejar el colegio.**

d) **Voy a buscar un trabajo.**

e) **Voy a ir a la universidad.**

5 marks

14 Put the following sentences about daily routine in the correct order.

a) **Me acuesto a las diez.**

b) **Me visto y desayuno.**

c) **Me levanto y me ducho en el cuarto de baño.**

d) **Me despierto a las siete menos cuarto.**

e) **Después del colegio, descanso en casa antes de hacer mis deberes.**

f) **Veo la televisión después de hacer mis deberes.**

6 marks

15 Read the text and say which of the sentences are true or false.

Me llamo Rafa y vivo en Murcia con mi madre. Mis padres están divorciados. Mi padre vive en el oeste de España con mi madrastra y mi hermanastro. Tengo catorce años y me gusta el fútbol, pero no me gusta nada el baloncesto. Me gustaría tener una hermana.

a) Rafa lives with his mum.　　T / F

b) He has a brother.　　T / F

c) He is 14 years old.　　T / F

d) He hates football.　　T / F

4 marks

16 Fill the gaps with the words below.

clásica	prefiere	tengo	irá	escuchar	el piano	compositor

Me encanta mi tiempo libre y a) .... **muchos pasatiempos. Primero,**

me gusta mucho b) .... **música y sobre todo me interesa la música**

c) .... **. Mi d)** .... **favorito es Mozart. También**

toco e) .... **, aunque en mi opinión es muy difícil de aprender. Mi**

hermana f) .... **la música pop y en octubre g)** ....

7 marks

a un concierto de Pink.

17 Translate this email to your brother from his Spanish penfriend.

> Vivo en una casa grande y moderna con mi familia. Tengo dos hermanas y un hermano. Mi hermano es bajo pero inteligente. Mis hermanas son divertidas, pero a veces me ponen de los nervios. Soy atlético y juego al voleibol todos los lunes por la tarde.

....

....

....

....

10 marks

18 Write these activities that you can do with technology in the first person present and preterite tense.

a) **Mandar mensajes** ....

b) **Buscar información** ....

c) **Compartir fotos** ....

d) **Hacer compras en línea** ....

8 marks

19 You are on a school trip to Valencia and you read this notice at the local sports centre.

Deportes	Detalles
Natación	Concurso con premios.
Baloncesto	Clases para adultos.
Boxeo	Clases para menores de 18 años.
Fútbol	Concurso de liga.
Pelota	Concurso para adultos.
Baile	Es importante no olvidar los zapatos de baile.

Answer the questions below.

a) Which is the best sport for adults? ....

b) Which is the sport with prizes? ....

c) What age do you need to be to do boxing? ....

d) What are you asked to bring to the dance sessions? ....

4 marks

20 Read and do the exercise below.

> Vivo en el centro de Xalapa, una ciudad universitaria en México. En general me gusta mucho mi pueblo, pero hay unas cosas que se deberían mejorar. Primero deben construir más zonas peatonales así habrá menos contaminación. También me gustaría ver menos basura en la calle, creo que la gente no es responsable y eso me molesta mucho.

Find the following Spanish phrases in the text.

a) university town ....

b) to improve ....

c) pedestrian areas ....

d) there will be ....

☐ 4 marks

21 Translate the sentences into Spanish.

a) I get on well with my family.

b) I like to watch science fiction films.

c) We went to the cinema last Friday.

d) My brother is very clever and funny.

☐ 8 marks

22 Match the two halves of the items below.

un helado de	**pescado**
un té	**leche**
un pastel de	**vainilla**
un sándwich	**chocolate**
una tarta	**con limón**
un café con	**albaricoque**
un mousse de	**de jamón**
la sopa de	**de café**

☐ 8 marks

23 Look at these sentences and decide if **mucho / mucha / muchos / muchas** or **muy** fits.

a) **Hay** .... **personas en la biblioteca hoy.**

b) **Hay** .... **ruido en la calle porque hay demasiados atascos.**

c) **En el pasado había** .... **basura en el parque, pero ahora está mejor.**

d) Es _____ divertido ir a la playa, aunque hay _____ gente.

e) Tengo _____ trabajo y estoy _____ estresado.

7 marks

24 Complete the following paragraph about Eduardo's future plans using the words from the box.

los exámenes	ir	universidad	ser	al colegio	estudiar

En este momento va _____ y en junio va a aprobar _____. Él va

a _____ a la _____ para _____ ciencias.

Quisiera _____ médico.

6 marks

25 Read what Luis says below and answer the questions in English.

Me llamo Luis y trabajo como bombero, pero en el futuro quisiera ser futbolista porque creo que sería bien pagado y muy emocionante.

a) What job does Luis do now?   b) What job would he like to do and why?

2 marks

26 Write sentences to describe Jim and Gustavo's holidays *in the past*.

Person	Place	Who with	Transport	How long	Accommodation	Activity
Sandra	the mountains	cousin	plane	five days	hotel	hiking
Jim	the beach	friends	car	one week	youth hostel	sunbathing
Gustavo	Rome	alone	train	one month	friend's house	to learn Italian

Example: **Sandra: Fui a las montañas con mi prima, fui en avión y fui por cinco días. Me quedé en un hotel, e hice senderismo.**

Jim: _____

_____

_____

Gustavo: _____

_____

_____

10 marks

27 When does each person have their birthday?

a) **El cumpleaños de Marta es el quince de julio.** ....

b) **El cumpleaños de Sara es el diecisiete de noviembre.** ....

c) **El cumpleaños de Antonio es el primero de febrero.** ....

d) **El cumpleaños de José es el treinta y uno de enero.** ....

e) **El cumpleaños de Ana es el veinticinco de marzo.** ....

5 marks

28 Read this interview with Selma about the Olympics then choose the correct response.

a) **¿Cuál deporte te interesa más?** **Me interesa más la vela.**

i) swimming **ii)** sailing **iii)** horse-riding

b) **¿Cuándo vas a ver los Juegos?** **Voy a ver los Juegos después del colegio.**

i) after school **ii)** after homework **iii)** before school

c) **¿Dónde vas a ver los Juegos?** **Voy a ver los Juegos en la casa de mi abuela.**

i) at his aunt's house **ii)** at his granddad's house **iii)** at his grandma's house

3 marks

29 Match up these sentences so they make sense.

Recibo 10	**ayudar en casa.**
El año pasado	**iré a la universidad.**
En dos meses	**a mi perro.**
Es importante	**libras cada mes.**
Debería pasear	**visité España.**
Gasto mi dinero en	**revistas y maquillaje.**

6 marks

30 Translate these sentences into Spanish.

a) I am 12 years old.

b) My birthday is 25 September.

c) I like chocolate but I don't like exams.

d) The church is small.

8 marks

31 Read the paragraph which describes Raúl's feelings about his previous life in the countryside and fill in the gaps with the appropriate tense – present or imperfect.

a) _____ (tener) mucha suerte porque vivo en la ciudad. Anteriormente

b) _____ (vivir) en el campo y c) _____ (ser) muy aislado, no

d) _____ (haber) ni tiendas ni instalaciones deportivas. ¡Lo malo fue

que mis amigos e) _____ (estar) muy lejos, y los fines de semana me

f) _____ (quedar) en casa y no g) _____ (hacer) nada! Ahora

estoy más contento porque h) _____ (vivir) a 10 minutos del centro y

todo está cerca.

8 marks

32 Answer the following questions in Spanish.

a) ¿Cómo se llama tu colegio?   b) ¿Dónde se halla tu colegio?

c) ¿Cuántos alumnos hay en tu colegio?   d) ¿A qué hora empiezan las clases?

e) ¿Qué haces durante la hora de comer?   f) ¿Cómo es tu uniforme?

g) ¿Cuál es tu asignatura preferida?   h) ¿A qué hora terminan las clases?

8 marks

33 Fill in the grid with the missing first-person verbs.

	Present	Preterite	Immediate future	Conditional
hacer	a)	b)	Voy a hacer	haría
ir	voy	c)	d)	iría
tener	e)	tuve	f)	g)

7 marks

34 Match up these items of clothing.

una camiseta	dress
una sudadera	shoes
una corbata	T-shirt
un vestido	sweatshirt
un abrigo	tie
unos zapatos	coat

6 marks

35 Translate this email from your Colombian friend.

> Vivo en un pequeño pueblo en el norte de Colombia. Mi casa está al lado del parque. Los sábados me gusta ir en bicicleta con mis amigos. Recientemente nadé en la piscina con mi hermana. En el futuro me gustaría vivir en el sur de España en Málaga porque siempre hay mucho que hacer.

10 marks

36 Read the dialogue and complete the statements in English.

Pepe: ¿Hay un mercado cerca de aquí? Quiero comprar comida típica.

Marisol: Sí, está a diez minutos a pie, toma la primera calle a la derecha, y al final de la calle hay una comisaría y el mercado está al lado.

Muy bien, gracias.

¿De dónde eres?

Soy de los Estados Unidos.

¡Hablas muy bien el español! ¿Qué haces en Málaga?

Pues estoy de visita con mi universidad.

¿Cuál es tu opinión de Málaga?

Pues, me encanta todo, lo único es que ¡no me gusta el calor!…

a) Pepe wants to buy ....

b) He needs to take the ....

c) Next to the market there is a ....

d) He is from ....

e) He doesn't like the ....

5 marks

37 Fill in the gaps with the words from the box.

tres	diez	comparto	un televisor	genial

En casa tengo a) .... **habitaciones. Tenemos b)** ....

dormitorios. Yo c) .... **mi dormitorio con mi hermano. En mi**

dormitorio, hay (d) .... **y un ordenador. Es e)** ....

5 marks

38 In Spanish, write where in the town you would do these activities.

a) **Nadar**

b) **Ver un partido de fútbol**

c) **Aprender sobre la historia local**

d) **Pasear al perro**

4 marks

39 Rewrite the sentence adding a connective, a frequency word, an intensifier and an opinion.

Me gusta ver los dibujos animados.

4 marks

40 Read these sentences and say if the statements are positive or negative.

a) **El uniforme es incómodo.**

b) **Hay una nueva piscina.**

c) **Los profesores son aburridos.**

d) **Tengo muchos amigos en el colegio.**

e) **Soy fuerte en matemáticas.**

f) **No hay bastantes ordenadores.**

g) **Los vestuarios son modernos.**

h) **Los edificios son viejos.**

8 marks

41 Put these daily routines into the correct order.

a) **Desayuno cereales y leche.**

b) **Salgo de casa.**

c) **Me despierto temprano.**

d) **Me acuesto a las 9.**

e) **Ceno salchichas.**

f) **Me levanto a las 7 y media.**

g) **Me divierto en la clase de teatro.**

7 marks

42 Rearrange the following words to make a sentence about holidays.

Siempre	a	porque	hace	Grecia	voy	calor

1 mark

43 In Spanish, name three things you can do online.

a)

b)

c)

3 marks

44 Jaime is talking about sport. Put the five sentences into order, from his favourite sport to his least favourite activity.

No soporto la natación porque odio mojarme.

Además, me mola el tenis y lo juego con mi hermano dos o tres veces por semana.

No me gusta nada el rugby porque me aburre muchísimo.

Me apasiona el fútbol, es mi deporte favorito. Juego al fútbol a diario.

Me gusta mucho la equitación, pero prefiero el tenis.

5 marks

45 Translate the following into Spanish:

I always watch TV with my parents on a Sunday. I love documentaries, but my dad likes the news.

3 marks

46 For each country write the nationality.

a) **España** .... b) **Inglaterra** ....

c) **Francia** .... d) **Alemania** ....

4 marks

47 In Spanish, write the countries these capital cities belong to:

a) **Cardiff** .... b) **Edimburgo** ....

c) **Roma** .... d) **Washington D.C.** ....

4 marks

48 Correct the following sentences by changing the word in italics.

a) **La fruta y las legumbres son *malas* para la salud.**

b) **Desayuno *tostadas* con leche.**

c) **Mi *legumbre* preferida es una manzana.**

d) **Hay que *beber* mucha ensalada.**

e) **No hay que *hacer* muchos cigarrillos.**

5 marks

Pronunciation Guide

Guía de pronunciación

Spanish pronunciation is straightforward. There are, however, some rules to follow.

Vowels	Pronounced...	Examples
a	'aaah' like the 'a' in the English word 'spa'	**araña** (spider), **mala** (bad), **nada** (nothing)
e	'eh' like the 'e' in the English word 'set'	**elefante** (elephant), **eso** (that), **bebé** (baby)
i and y (and)	'ee' like the 'ee' sound in the words 'we' or 'me'	**isla** (island), **iglesia** (church), **hija** (daughter)
o	'oh' like the 'o' sound in the English word 'go'	**ocho** (eight), **oso** (bear), **yo** (I)
u	'ooo' like the 'oo' sound in the English word 'boot'	**uva** (grape), **luna** (moon), **única** (unique)

Consonants	Pronounced...	Examples
h	silent	**hormiga** (ant), **hotel** (hotel), **hola** (hello)
j	h many 'j' words are cognates	**junio** (June), **justicia** (justice), **jaguar** (jaguar)
ñ	'ni' like the 'ni' sound in the English word 'junior'	**año** (year), **piña** (pineapple), **mañana** (tomorrow / morning)
q	'k' like in the English word 'keep' q is always followed by 'u', which is silent.	**qué** (what), **quién** (who), **queso** (cheese)
r	softly when in the middle of a word as in the English word 'water'	**actriz** (actress), **caro** (expensive), **sombrero** (hat)
	trilled like the English word 'brrrrr' when at the beginning of a Spanish word	**ratón** (mouse), **rico** (rich), **roto** (broken)
z	'th' like the sound 'th' in the English word 'theatre'	**zapato** (shoe), **zorro** (fox), **zanahoria** (carrot)

Letter combinations	Pronounced...	Examples
ce and ci	the 'c' is pronounced 'th'	**cena** (supper), **cien** (one hundred), **gracias** (thank you)
ch	'ch' like the English word 'church'	**chocolate** (chocolate), **chiringuito** (beach bar), **churro** (churro)
ge and gi	the 'g' is pronounced 'h' when followed by 'e' or 'i' otherwise the 'g' is a hard sound as in 'good'	**geografía** (geography), **girasol** (sunflower), **gente** (people), **gorra** (cap)
ll	'y' like in the English word 'yellow'	**me llamo** (I am called), **amarillo** (yellow), **llave** (key)
rr	trilled like in the English word 'brrrrr'	**burro** (donkey), **perro** (dog), **arreglar** (to fix)

Answers

Page 5 Quick Test
1. Me llamo_____y tengo _____años.
2. ¿Cómo te llamas? ¿Cuántos años tienes?
3. hermanastra
4. Hello! My name is Alicia and I am nearly 13. My birthday is on the 25th of August. I live in Murcia with my parents and my three siblings; one brother and two sisters. My brother is called Diego and he is 10 years old. My sisters are called Maria and Luisa and they are 7 years old. They are twins.

Page 7 Quick Test
1. Tengo el pelo largo, rubio y rizado y los ojos marrones.
2. Mi hermana es baja.
3. No tengo mascota. / No tengo animales.
4. Mi hermano tiene dos gatos.

Page 9 Quick Test
1. Vivo en una casa en un pueblo en el este de Inglaterra.
2. bathroom – masculine; kitchen – feminine; garden – masculine
3. lejos de
4. Comparto mi dormitorio con mi hermana.

Page 11 Quick Test
1. un escritorio, una cama, una silla, un ordenador
2. un escritorio – masculine; una cama – feminine; una silla – feminine; un ordenador – masculine
3. Mi escritorio está al lado del armario.
4. Ayudo a mi madre cada día.

Page 13 Quick Test
1. **b)** un melocotón
2. Como manzanas cada día.
3. I eat watermelon because I like the taste.
4. **c)** Los guisantes son negros.

Page 15 Quick Test
1. **d)** una ensalada mixta
2. De postre, quisiera / me gustaría un helado de fresa.
3. Add a little sugar to the coffee.

Page 17 Quick Test
1. **b)** en la piscina.
2. Me flipa el baloncesto pero no soporto el fútbol.
3. I play football every day but I never play guitar.
4. **d)** el patinaje

Page 19 Quick Test
1. **d)** los dientes.
2. Estoy enfermo (masculine) / enferma (feminine), me duelen la garganta y la cabeza.
3. I don't eat a lot of greasy food because it is bad for your health.
4. **b)** Voy a fumar.

1. **a)** morado [1]
   b) verde [1]
   c) gris [1]
   d) rosa [1]
2. Uno, dos, tres, cuatro, cinco, seis, siete, ocho, nueve, diez, once, doce, trece, catorce, quince, dieciséis, diecisiete, dieciocho, diecinueve, veinte. [20]

3. lunes, martes, miércoles, jueves, viernes, sábado, domingo [7]
4. **a)** febrero [1]
   b) abril [1]
   c) junio [1]
   d) agosto [1]
   e) octubre [1]
   f) diciembre [1]
5. **a)** tres [1]
   b) siete [1]
   c) doce [1]
   d) catorce [1]
   e) seis [1]
   f) veinte [1]
   g) trece [1]
   h) cuatro [1]
   i) diez [1]
   j) dieciocho [1]
   k) once [1]
   l) quince [1]
6. veinticinco ——— 25 [1]
   treinta y siete ——— 37 [1]
   cuarenta y dos ——— 42 [1]
   setenta y nueve ——— 79 [1]
   ochenta y tres ——— 83 [1]
7. **a)** veintinueve [1]
   b) cincuenta y uno [1]
   c) setenta y dos [1]
   d) ochenta y seis [1]
   e) noventa y cuatro [1]
8. **a)** Es la una [1]
   b) Son las siete. [1]
   c) Son las ocho y diez. [1]
   d) Son las diez y cuarto. [1]
   e) Son las once y media. [1]
   f) Son las cinco menos cuarto. [1]
   g) Son las siete menos cinco. [1]
9. **a)** Son las dos. [1]
   b) Son las tres y veinte. [1]
   c) Son las seis y cuarto. [1]
   d) Son las nueve y media. [1]
   e) Son las nueve menos cuarto. [1]
   f) Son las doce menos diez. [1]
10. ¿Qué fecha ——— es hoy? [1]
   ¿Cuánto ——— cuesta? [1]
   ¿Quién ——— nació en septiembre? [1]
   ¿Dónde hace calor ——— en invierno? [1]
   ¿Cómo se dice ——— 'miércoles' en inglés? [1]
   ¿Cuándo es ——— tu cumpleaños? [1]
11. **a)** hace mucho calor [1]
   b) hace sol [1]
   c) hace mal tiempo [1]
   d) llueve [1]
   e) hace frío [1]
   f) hace viento [1]
   g) hay niebla [1]
   h) hace buen tiempo [1]
   i) hay una temperatura de 30 grados [1]

Page 22
1. **a)** ¿Cómo te llamas? ——— Me llamo Ana. [1]
   b) ¿Cuántos años tienes? ——— Tengo trece años. [1]
   c) ¿Tienes hermanos? ——— No, soy hijo único. [1]

d) ¿Tienes mascotas? —— Sí, tengo un perro. [1]

e) ¿Cómo se llama tu padre? —— Él se llama Felipe. [1]

2. a) años [1]

b) una, hermanos [2]

c) marrones, castaño [2]

d) cariñosos [1]

e) gato, se llama [2]

3. Me llamo Marco. Mi cumpleaños es el treinta y uno de mayo y nací en dos mil ocho (or nací el treinta y uno de mayo, dos mil ocho). Vivo en Madrid. No tengo hermanos, soy hijo único. Tengo los ojos azules y el pelo corto y negro. No tengo mascotas / animales. [7]

Me llamo Elena. Mi cumpleaños es el once de julio y nací en dos mil nueve (or nací el once de julio, dos mil nueve). Vivo en Mérida. Tengo una hermana y un hermano. Tengo los ojos verdes y el pelo largo y castaño. Tengo un conejo y tiene tres años. [7]

Page 23

1. a) el salón [1]

b) el dormitorio / la habitación [1]

c) la cocina [1]

d) el ático [1]

e) el cuarto de baño [1]

f) el armario [1]

g) la cama [1]

h) la silla [1]

i) el escritorio [1]

j) el ordenador [1]

2. En mi dormitorio —— hay un ordenador. [1]

La televisión está sobre —— mi escritorio. [1]

Comparto mi dormitorio —— con mi hermana. [1]

Hay dos sillones —— en el salón. [1]

3. Vivo **en un apartamento** grande en una **ciudad** pequeña en el **sur** de Inglaterra. Me **encanta** mi ciudad. En mi casa hay **diez** habitaciones, pero no hay **jardín**. En mi **dormitorio** hay un **ordenador**. Es genial. En el dormitorio de mi hermano **hay** una consola. [10]

Page 24

1. Three from: vegetables, chicken, salad, chocolate cake [3]

2. Sopa de tomate, Tortilla Española, Macedonia de frutas, either tea or coffee [4]

Page 25

1. a) toothache — B [1]

b) headache — E [1]

c) sore feet — D [1]

d) backache — A [1]

e) stomach ache — C [1]

2. a) la equitación [1]

b) el ciclismo [1]

c) el tenis [1]

d) el fútbol [1]

e) la vela [1]

3. a) malo [1]

b) bueno [1]

c) bueno [1]

d) malo [1]

e) malo [1]

f) malo [1]

g) bueno [1]

h) bueno [1]

Pages 26–41 **Revise Questions**

Page 27 Quick Test

1. c) la historia

2. Me gusta la historia porque es divertida.

3. I don't like maths because the teacher is boring.

4. c) Me encanta el inglés porque es inútil.

Page 29 Quick Test

1. b) está prohibido

2. Hay que llevar una chaqueta negra.

3. Classes start at a quarter to nine.

4. c) No me gusta el uniforme porque es cómodo.

Page 31 Quick Test

1. Any three from: abogado / abogada; actor / actriz; director / directora de una empresa; diseñador / diseñadora de videojuegos; diseñador / diseñadora web; enfermero / enfermera; entrenador / entrenadora; ingeniero / ingeniera; médico / médica; peluquero / peluquera; piloto / pilota; profesor / profesora; traductor / traductora; veterinario / veterinaria

2. in a hospital

3. Any of the people in **1.** that may work in an office.

4. You must / It is necessary to work.

Page 33 Quick Test

1. Soy fuerte en; Me interesa(n); Me apasiona(n); Me flipa(n); Soy / hincha de

2. Health and friends

3. I'm going to study maths.

4. Any answer from the ambitions section on p. 33.

Page 35 Quick Test

1. (no) Toco un instrumento.

2. Me gusta / no me gusta (any opinion phrase) la música clásica.

3. Me encanta la música pop porque es rítmica.

4. Me gustaría

Page 37 Quick Test

1. El parque (m) / la playa (f) / el centro comercial (m) / la biblioteca (f)

2. a) al, **b)** al, **c)** a la

3. ¿Quieres / te apetece / te gustaría ver una película mañana?

4. a) película de historia

b) dibujo animado

c) ciencia ficción

Page 39 Quick Test

1. películas, son

2. Nunca veo / miro programas de música.

3. Me gustan las telenovelas porque son emocionantes.

4. veo, vemos

Page 41 Quick Test

1. You can / one can

2. hay, ciberacoso

3. chateo, hago, juego

4. Siempre veo las noticias porque son informativas.

Pages 42–45 **Review Questions**

Page 42

1. a) mi madre [1]

b) mi tío [1]

c) mi abuelo [1]

d) mi abuela [1]

e) mi hermana [1]

2. Tengo el pelo —— rubio. | I have blond hair. [2]

Soy —— alta y delgada. | I am tall and thin. [2]

Tengo —— trece años. | I am 13 years old. [2]

Tengo los ojos —— azules. | I have blues eyes. [2]

3. a) ¿Cómo te llamas? [1]

b) ¿Cuántos años tienes? [1]

c) ¿Cuándo es tu cumpleaños? [1]

d) ¿Tienes hermanos? [1]

e) ¿Dónde vives? [1]

f) ¿Tienes mascotas / animales? [1]

4. Me **llamo** Alison. **Tengo** doce años, pero mi hermana **tiene** ocho años. Tengo el **pelo** largo y los **ojos** marrones. No tengo **perro** (or any animal other than a cat). Mi gato **se llama** Pedro. [7]

5. **a)** Tengo quince años. [1]
b) Mi cumpleaños es el seis de mayo. [1]
c) Tengo el pelo corto y los ojos verdes. [1]
d) Tengo un conejo blanco. [1]

Page 43

1. **a)** Vivo **en** Londres. [1]
b) Vivimos **en** el norte de Inglaterra. [1]
c) Mi amiga vive **en una** casa grande. [1]
d) Mis primos viven **en un** apartamento. [1]
2. **a)** Vivo en una casa pequeña. [1]
b) En mi casa hay ocho habitaciones. / Hay ocho habitaciones en mi casa. [1]
c) No tengo ordenador en mi dormitorio. / En mi dormitorio no tengo ordenador. [1]
d) El televisor está sobre la mesa. [1]
3. **a)** No tengo ordenador. [1]
b) Mi dormitorio no es grande. [1]
c) No tenemos jardín. [1]
d) No lavo los platos a menudo. [1]
e) Mi hermana no tiene portátil en su dormitorio. [1]
4. **a)** Vivo en una casa pequeña en el sur de Inglaterra. [1]
b) En casa tenemos nueve habitaciones. [1]
c) Paso la aspiradora a menudo. [1]
d) Friego los platos a menudo, pero es aburrido. [1]

Page 44

1. **a)** una fresa [1]
b) un limón [1]
c) un melocotón [1]
d) una piña [1]
e) una manzana [1]
2. **a)** Tomo la sopa de **tomate**. [1]
b) De postre he elegido **un helado**. [1]
c) Para beber voy a tomar **un zumo de fruta**. [1]
d) ¿Dónde están **los aseos?** [1]
3. Carne (meat): **d)** unas albóndigas, **e)** un filete [2]
Verduras (vegetables): **a)** unos champiñones, **h)** unos guisantes [2]
Postres (desserts): **c)** una tarta de fresa, **g)** un helado de limón [2]
Fruta (fruit): **b)** las peras, **f)** unos plátanos [2]

Page 45

1. e); c); b); a); d) [5]
2. **a)** No como nunca helado porque **es malo para la salud**. [1]
b) Hago deporte muy a menudo porque **quiero mantenerme en forma**. [1]
c) Voy al dentista porque **me duelen los dientes**. [1]
3. **a)** **Hay que** tomar ensalada. [1]
b) **Hay que** beber agua. [1]
c) **No hay que** comer mucho chocolate. [1]
d) **No hay que** beber mucho café. [1]
e) **Hay que** hacer deporte. [1]

Pages 46–49 **Practice Questions**

Page 46

a) F [1]
b) A [1]
c) C [1]
d) E [1]

2. **a)** útil [1]
b) genial [1]
c) difícil [1]
d) débil en deporte [1]

Page 47

1. **a)** profesora [1]
b) enfermero / médico [1]
c) cartero [1]
d) bombera [1]
2.

Masculine	Feminine
peluquero	peluquera
cantante	cantante
actor	actriz
hombre de negocio	mujer de negocios
médico	médica
abogado	abogada
ingeniero	ingeniera

[14]

3. **a)** cortés [1]
b) emocionante [1]
c) rico [1]
4. **[Award 2 marks per sentence, 1 mark for a correct verb and 1 mark for a suitable infinitive or noun.]** [6]

Page 48

1. **a)** a la [1]
b) al [1]
c) al [1]
d) a la [1]
2. trece; animados; Dumbo; padres; telenovelas; tontas [6]
3. d); a); e); f); b); c) [6]
4. ¿Quieres ir al cine el domingo?
¿Qué ponen?
Ponen la película *Toy Story 2*.
¿A qué hora empieza la película?
A las cinco.
Muy bien! Nos vemos en el cine. [6]

Page 49

1. **a)** Ver [1]
b) Chatear [1]
c) Descargar [1]
d) Buscar [1]
e) Leer [1]
f) Jugar [1]
2. **a)** verb ——— veo, son [2]
b) adjective ——— impresionantes [1]
c) noun ——— documentales, animales [2]
d) connective ——— porque [1]
e) intensifier ——— muy [1]
3. Mi programa favorito es____ porque es _____. [2]
4. Any two, e.g.
Es una distracción.
Puede ser una pérdida de tiempo.
Hay mucha violencia.
Hay mucho ciberacoso.
Hay demasiadas noticias falsas.
Se puede encontrar personas peligrosas. [2]
5. **a)** Siempre chateo con mis amigos. [1]
b) A menudo mando mensajes a mis amigos en otros países / el extranjero. [1]
c) A veces descargo mi música favorita. [1]
d) Me encanta ver las películas de ciencia ficción con mi hermano. [1]

Page 51 Quick Test
1. estos pantalones negros
2. este abrigo marrón de cuero
3. Me gusta **llevar botas negras** porque son cómodas.
4. ¿Cuánto es / cuánto cuesta / Cuál es el precio?

Page 53 Quick Test
1. Recibo _____ libras esterlinas / euros.
2. Gasto mi dinero / ahorro mi dinero.
3. Trabaja en un café.
4. Ayudo mucho en casa el fin de semana.

Page 55 Quick Test
1. tranquilo, sucio, bonito
2. Prefiero vivir en el pueblo / la ciudad.
3. mucha gente (it is a singular noun)
4. There is a lot to do.

Page 57 Quick Test
1. el cine; centro comercial; puede, el mercado / el supermercado / la frutería
2. Hay muchas piscinas.
   No hay suficientes parques.
3. I would like to see more green areas and less traffic in my town. [Note word order has been changed to make it sound more English.]
4. Quiero

Page 59 Quick Test
1. España; español
2. Voy con mis padres / amigos etc.
3. es más rápido
4. Fui a la costa en julio. [Note the time element can be placed either at start or end of sentence.]

Page 61 Quick Test
1. Me relajo en la playa con mis padres.
2. Quiero / me gustaría / quisiera una habitación doble con vista del mar para una semana.
3. ¿Te gusta sacar / tomar fotos?
4. hace, piscina

Page 63 Quick Test
1. Tengo que
2. Hay demasiado tráfico en el centro de Londres. / En el centro de Londres hay demasiado tráfico. / There is too much traffic in the centre of London.
3. No debería malgastar agua. [**'debo'** also possible]
4. mucho, muy

Page 65 Quick Test
1. Debo / debería respetar a los demás / otras personas / I must / should respect others / other people.
2. Debo apreciar lo que tengo. [The second verb must be infinitive.] / I must appreciate what I have.
3. Me preocupa mucho el calentamiento global.
   I am really worried about global warming. / Global warming really worries me.
4. Any three: buen / mayor / próximo / último / nuevo.

Page 66
1. a) D [1]
   b) E [1]
   c) F [1]
   d) A [1]
   e) G [1]

2. a) fácil [1]
   b) inútil [1]
   c) divertido [1]
   d) aburrido [1]

Page 67
1. a) un médico / una médica / un enfermero / una enfermera [1]
   b) anyone who works in an office [1]
   c) anyone who works in a shop [1]
2. No need to use un / una [1]
3. a) En cuatro años [1]
   b) En dos años [1]
   c) En el futuro [1]
4. a) Soy fuerte en [1]
   b) Soy aficionado de [1]
   c) No me interesa el / la [1]
5. Él es **diseñador web** y trabaja en **una oficina**. Le gusta mucho su trabajo porque es verdaderamente **dinámico**. Puede **crear** nuevos sitios web. Para ser un bueno compañero de trabajo es necesario ser **inspirador**. [5]

Page 68
1. a) toco [1]
   b) toca [1]
   c) tocar [1]
   d) tocar [1]
   e) tocamos [1]
2. a) Me gusta escuchar la música clásica porque es relajante. [1]
   b) Mi grupo favorito es americano. [1]
   c) Prefiero escuchar la música salsa porque es rítmica. [1]
   d) Ayer fui a un concierto de rock. [Time can go at start or end of sentence.] [1]
   e) ¿Te gustaría escuchar la música en vivo? [1]
3. a) al [1]
   b) a las [1]
   c) al [1]
   d) al [1]
   e) a la [1]
4. Hola me **llamo** Benji y me gustan mucho las películas de **ciencia** ficción. Creo que **son** emocionantes y los efectos especiales son **geniales**. Fui al cine el **sábado** pasado, ¡lo pasé muy bien! [5]

Page 69
1. a) Telerrealidad [1]
   b) Documental [1]
   c) Telenovela [1]
   d) Dibujo animado [1]
   e) Programa / emisión de deportes [1]
   f) Noticias / el telediario [1]
2. a) Siempre veo las noticias porque son informativas. [Plural of verb needed.] [2]
   b) A menudo mi padre ve documentales sobre la historia. [Time element can be at start or end of sentence.] [2]
   c) ¿Te gusta ver las telenovelas? [2]
   d) El domingo voy a ver una serie de Netflix con mi madre. [2]
   e) Prefiero ver dibujos animados porque son graciosos e entretenidos. [2]
3. a) time phrase —— el fin de semana [1]
   b) infinitive verb —— ver [1]
   c) opinion phrase —— me encanta / creo que [1]
   d) adjective —— emocionantes [1]
   e) intensifier —— muy [1]
   f) noun —— emisiones de deportes [1]
4. Any three, for example:

Mando mensajes.	I send messages.
Chateo con mis amigos.	I chat with friends.
Compruebo mis correos electrónicos	I check my emails.
Juego a los videojuegos.	I play video games.
Hago clases de escuela en línea.	I do online school classes
Descargo música.	I download music.

Hago las compras en línea.	I do online shopping.
Veo vídeos.	I watch videos.
Leo blogs.	I read blogs.
Comparto fotos.	I share photos.
Busco información.	I look for information.
Pongo mi página al día.	I update my page.
Hago arreglos sociales.	I make social arrangements. [3]

5. a) mucho [5]
    b) muchas [1]
    c) mucho [1]
    d) mucha [1]
    e) muchos [1]

Pages 70–73 **Practice Questions**

Page 70
1. a) Llevo una camisa blanca. [1]
    b) Llevo una chaqueta negra de cuero. [1]
    c) Prefiero llevar ropa de moda. [1]
    d) Me gustaría llevar vaqueros al colegio. [1]
2. a) Me gustan mis botas marrones. [1]
    b) El fin de semana prefiero llevar mis zapatillas de deporte blancos. [1]
    c) Ayer compré una sudadera amarilla y gris. [1]
3. a) Quiero / me gustaría comprar [1]
    b) número [**talla** is for clothing] [1]
    c) color [1]
    d) cuánto son / cuánto cuestan [1]
4. Cada semana recibo cinco libras y compro revistas de moda. [1]

Page 71
1. a) Polideportivo [1]
    b) centro comercial [1]
    c) museo [1]
    d) mercado / supermercado [1]
    e) estadio [1]
    f) biblioteca [1]
2. a) La vida <u>puede</u> <u>ser</u> estresante. (T) [2]
    b) Se <u>puede</u> <u>respirar</u> aire limpio. (C) [2]
    c) Siempre <u>hay</u> mucho que <u>hacer.</u> (T) [2]
    d) <u>Tengo</u> que <u>esperar</u> mucho tiempo para el autobús. (C) [2]
    e) Las vistas <u>son</u> increíbles y <u>hay</u> mucha tranquilidad. (C) [2]
3. a) sigue todo recto [1]
    b) toma la calle a la derecha [1]
    c) toma la calle a la izquierda [1]
    d) toma la primera calle a la derecha [1]
    e) toma la segunda calle a la izquierda [1]
    f) cruza la plaza [1]

Page 72
1. a) español [1]
    b) Alemania [1]
    c) los Estados Unidos [1]
    d) inglés [1]
    e) Italia [1]
    f) portugués [1]
2. a) voy (P) [1]
    b) Vamos (P) [1]
    c) Hago (P) [1]
    d) Fui (PA) [1]
    e) Me quedé (PA) [1]
    f) Voy a ir (F) [1]
    g) Prefiero (P) [1]
3. a) Voy a Francia en barco y en coche. [1]
    b) Vamos con mis abuelos. [1]
    c) Normalmente me quedo en un albergue juvenil en Irlanda. [1]
    d) El año pasado fui a España y visité muchos lugares / sitios de interés. [2]

e) Hice ciclismo y jugué al fútbol en la playa. [2]
f) Me gustaría quedarme en un hotel de cinco estrellas, pero es caro. [2]
    [Parts d)–f) 1 mark for each correct verb.]

Page 73
1. a) i) to help [1]
        ii) to support [1]
        iii) to be [1]
        iv) to do / make [1]
    b) i) ayudo / ayudé / voy a ayudar [3]
        ii) apoyo / apoyé / voy a apoyar [3]
        iii) soy / fui / voy a ser [3]
        iv) hago / hice / voy a hacer [3]
2. Apreciar ———————— lo que tenemos. [1]
    Usar ———————— el transporte público. [1]
    Tomar ———————— interés en la política. [1]
    Ser ———————— responsable. [1]
    Donar ———————— ropa y comida. [1]
3. Intento ayudar a la gente sin techo. / I try to help homeless people. [2]
4. Me llamo Silvia y creo que todos deben ser responsables en cuanto a nuestra sociedad. Yo, por mi parte **tomo** mucho interés en la política e intento **escuchar** las noticias. Además,**uso** el transporte público o **voy** en bicicleta si puedo. Mi madre **es** miembro de un club ecologista y por eso **reciclamos** papel y botellas y **donamos** ropa y comida a las caridades para gente menos afortunada. [7]
5. Ayer usé el transporte público y mañana voy a reciclar papel en el colegio. [**Uso – usé**: past tense needed; **reciclo – reciclar** infinitive needed as it's an immediate future.] [2]

Pages 75–89 **Revise Questions**

Page 75 Quick Test
1. el, la, el, la
2. los caballos, los profesores, las ciudades, los actores
3. Hay unas gomas, unos bolígrafos, unos lápices, los estuches.
4. el día

Page 77 Quick Test
1. Los chicos bajos. Las asignaturas fáciles. Los bolígrafos naranja.
2. mucho ruido, muy repetitivo, muy impresionante, mucho turismo
3. más, que; menos, que; tan, como

Page 79 Quick Test
1. tengo; tiene; tengo
2. Tengo hambre.
3. está; es; estás; está

Page 81 Quick Test
1. I buy; it / he / she finishes; we watch; do you listen?
2. llego, llevamos, miran, escucha
3. beber, correr, terminar, vivir, aprender
4. they, we, he

Page 83 Quick Test
1. juego, vuelvo, quiero, empiezo
2. Jugamos al golf si volvemos temprano del colegio. / We play golf if we return / get home early from school.
3. Cuando llueve mucho no puedo salir y prefiero ver la tele.

Page 85 Quick Test
1. What activities do you do at the weekend?
2. Hace sol.
3. Vamos a **jugar al** voleibol el fin de semana.
4. I am going to go to the countryside with my parents on Sunday. I think it will be quiet but great.

Page 87 Quick Test

1. I don't see anyone / anybody at home.
2. Nunca bebo zumo por la mañana. / I never drink juice in the morning.
3. ¿Te gustan los perros?
4. Me **encantan** las matemáticas porque **son muy fáciles**.

Page 89 Quick Test

1. Ayer fui al parque donde jugué al fútbol.
2. Any preterite time phrase, ……. I worked with my mum in the garden, it was difficult!
3. llegar, jugar, entregar; add extra -u, i.e. ué
4. Ayer tuve una clase de español y aprendí muchos verbos.

Pages 90–93 **Review Questions**

Page 90

1. una chaqueta, unos pantalones / vaqueros, unos zapatos [3]
2. **a)** cotton [1]
   b) leather [1]
   c) wool [1]
3. Llevo unos vaqueros negros y un abrigo azul. / I am wearing black jeans and a blue coat. [2]
4. **a)** Me gustan estos zapatos marrones. [1]
   b) ¿Puedo probarlos / probar los zapatos? [1]
   c) ¿Cuánto son / cuánto cuestan? [1]
5. Any three, for example:
   Hago la compra.   I do the shopping.
   Ayudo en casa.   I help at home.
   Cuido a mi hermano menor.   I look after my younger brother.
   Trabajo en el jardín.   I work in the garden.
   Preparo la comida.   I prepare the food.
   Lavo los platos.   I wash the dishes.
   Arreglo mi dormitorio.   I tidy my bedroom.
   Pongo la mesa.   I set the table.
   Paseo al perro.   I walk the dog. [3]
6. Any two, for example: revistas, (magazines), videojuegos (videogames), ropa (clothes), maquillaje (make-up), caramelos (sweets), etc. [2]
7. Ayer trabajé en el jardín. [1]

Page 91

1. **a)** la piscina, la playa [1]
   b) la tienda de ropa, el centro comercial [1]
   c) el estadio [1]
   d) la estación de trenes [1]
   e) el cine [1]
2. **a)** mucho [1]
   b) tranquilo [1]
   c) genial [1]
   d) vida [1]
   e) instalaciones [1]
3. Dónde está el ————————— castillo. [1]
   Toma la primera calle ————————— a la derecha. [1]
   Está a cinco minutos ————————— a pie. [1]
   Sigue todo ————————— recto. [1]
   Está muy ————————— cerca. [1]

Page 92

1. **a)** España, **b)** Inglaterra, **c)** francés, **d)** alemán, **e)** Gales,
   f) los Estados Unidos [6]
2. **a)** Adónde [1]
   b) Con quién [1]
   c) Dónde [1]
   d) Por cuánto tiempo [1]
   e) Cómo [1]
   f) Te gusta
3. Javier: Voy a las montañas / con mis amigos / por una semana, / voy en coche / y me quedo en un albergue juvenil, / hago el senderismo. **[Each part of the sentence that gives information is worth 1 mark.]** [6]

Sara: Voy a Francia / con mi primo(a) / por un mes, / voy en tren / y me quedo en la casa de un amigo, / practico francés. **[Each part of the sentence that gives information is worth 1 mark.]** [6]
4. Es más rápido, es más cómodo / It is quicker / more quick, it is more comfortable [2]
5. Where did you go on holiday last year? [1]

Page 93

1. **a)** crisis [1]
   b) guerra [1]
   c) inundaciones [1]
2. Es necesario usar ——— el transporte público. [1]
   Es importante reciclar ——— papel y botellas en casa. [1]
   Se debe comprar ——— menos ropa. [1]
   Todo el mundo debe ayudar ——— a los menos afortunados. [1]
   Es esencial ser ——— responsable. [1]
   Es importante respetar ——— a los demás. [1]
3. **a)** It is necessary to use public transport. [1]
   b) It is important to recycle paper and bottles at home. [1]
4. **a)** Me gusta ayudar a mi vecino. [1]
   b) Quiero apoyar a las organizaciones benéficas / caridades. [1]
   c) Me preocupa la crueldad animal. [1]

Pages 94–97 **Practice Questions**

Page 94

1. **a)** la, **b)** el, **c)** el, **d)** la, **e)** las, **f)** la, **g)** los, **h)** el [8]
2. **a)** unos conejos blancos [1]
   b) unas casas azules [1]
   c) unas películas románticas [1]
   d) las madres estrictas [1]
   e) los lápices rosa (rosas) [1]
   f) los cursos difíciles [1]
3. **a)** Ben es más bajo que Eduardo. [1]
   b) roja, azules, negro, grises [4]

Page 95

1. **a)** tiene [1]
   b) tienen [1]
   c) tengo [1]
   d) tenemos [1]
2. **a)** está [1]
   b) es [1]
   c) estoy [1]
   d) está [1]
   e) son [1]
3. Tener frío —— to be cold [1]
   Tener prisa —— to be in a hurry [1]
   Tener ganas —— to feel like [1]
   Tener... años —— to be... (years old) [1]
   Tener hambre —— to be hungry [1]
   Tener calor —— to be hot [1]
   Tener sed —— to be thirsty [1]
4. llamo, vivo, está, nadamos, practico, toca, escucho, juego, ven [9]

Page 96

1. **a)** empieza [1]
   b) prefiero, prefiere [2]
   c) quiero, cuestan [2]
   d) juego, juega [2]
   e) podemos [1]
   f) llueve [1]
2. c) [You cannot say: Voy a la natación.] [1]
3. I am going to go to the cinema next Sunday, [1] it will be great. [1]
4. **a)** Pedro: En dos días [1] voy a viajar a Escocia [1] con mis tíos, [1] será emocionante. [1] **[1 mark for each: time, activity, who, with, opinion, up to a maximum of 4 marks.]**

b) Marcela: En agosto [1] voy a hacer un curso de inglés [1] sola [1], será difícil pero divertido.[1] **[1 mark for each: time, activity, who, with, opinion, up to a maximum of 4 marks.]** [4]

Page 97

1. **a)** Nunca veo la televisión. [1]
   b) No como ni carne ni pescado. [1]
   c) Nadie habla francés en mi familia. [1]
2. **a)** Me encanta el español. [1]
   b) Me gustan los perros. [1]
   c) ¿Te gustan los gatos? [1]
   d) A mi hermana le interesa el arte. [1]
   e) Me duele la cabeza. [1]
   f) ¿Qué te gusta hacer el sábado? [1]
3. Fui a la playa en julio, tomé el sol y jugué al voleibol, después, compré un helado y bebí una limonada. **[1 mark for each correct verb.]** [5]
4. fui, vi / vimos, fue, tuve, entregué, tuve, jugué, llegué [8]

Pages 99–105 **Revise Questions**

Page 99 Quick Test

1. I will eat less sugar in the future.
2. haré, tendré, podré, diré
3. **a)** Choose any time phrases for the future: en el futuro, mañana, en un mes, la semana próxima, etc.
   b) Choose any time phrase for the past: ayer, el sábado pasado etc.
   c) Choose any time phrase for the present: hoy, ahora, en este momento, etc.

Page 101 Quick Test

1. A pronoun which takes the place of an object. Positioned before the verb.
2. I eat them, Are you visiting me?, I am buying it, Did you do them?
3. I have a really good time. / I enjoy myself a lot.
4. Me llamo (I am called, my name is), me levanto (I get up), me despierto (I wake up)

Page 103 Quick Test

1. hablaba, veía, vivía, era
2. Any three: antes, anteriormente, en el pasado, cada día, todos los días.
3. Antes iba al parque, pero ahora voy al estadio.
4. What were you like when you were 10 years old?

Page 105 Quick Test

1. hablaría, viviría, tendría, haría
2. Would you like to live in Spain in the future?
3. No se debe comer chicle en clase.
4. Debería llegar a las nueve. [also 'debo']

Pages 106–107 **Practice Questions**

Page 106

1. Voy a hablar – I am going to speak. [1]
   Voy a jugar – I am going to play. [1]
   Voy a hacer – I am going to do / make. [1]
   Voy a tener – I am going to have. [1]
2. Any three from: En dos días, en el futuro, el año que viene, la semana próxima. [3]
3. **a)** Lo compro. [1]
   b) Mi madre los visita. [1]
4. Did you do your homework / prep? Yes I did it an hour ago. [2]
5. Me levanto nos levantamos, me llamo nos llamamos, me divierto nos divertimos **[Stem-changing verb; 1 mark for each correct verb.]** [6]
6. Mi amiga se llama Petra y estudiará en España el año que viene / el año próximo. **[1 mark for each correct verb.]** [3]

Page 107

1. preterite, imperfect, imperfect, preterite [4]
2. iba a la playa, trabajaba en una tienda, hacía muchos deportes + any imperfect time phrases [6]
3. Antes hacía clases de baile y me gustaban mucho. [1]
4. I would like. [1]
5. Mi casa ideal tendría una piscina y sería moderna. **[1 mark for each correct verb.]** [2]
6. Debería + any three, e.g.

escuchar en clase	listen in class
llegar a tiempo	arrive on time
entregar mis deberes a tiempo	hand in my homework on time
hacer mis deberes	do my homework
prestar atención	pay attention [3]

Pages 108–113 **Review Questions**

Page 108

1. **a)** la / una [1]
   b) el / un [1]
   c) las / unas [1]
   d) los / unos [1]
   e) el / un [1]
   f) las / unas [1]
2. **a)** zapatos rojos [1]
   b) un coche azul [1]
   c) una chaqueta negra y blanca [1]
   d) tiendas caras [1]
   e) botas marrones de cuero [1]
   f) un jersey naranja de lana [1]
3. **a)** Hay más habitantes en Glasgow que en Bilbao / la población es más grande.
   b) Hay más museos en Glasgow que en Bilbao.
   c) Hay más turistas en Glasgow que en Bilbao. [3]

Page 109

1. Mi abuelo tiene —— barba. [1]
   Tengo el pelo —— largo y rizado. [1]
   Madrid está —— en España. [1]
   ¿Cómo eres? —— Soy muy paciente. [1]
   ¿Cómo es tu profesor? —— Es muy estricto. [1]
   Cuántos años tienes? —— Trece. [1]
2. **a)** Juanita es baja y tiene el pelo rizado, es amable, tiene 12 años, su cumpleaños es el 19 de noviembre. **[1 mark for each correct verb.]** [5]
   b) Pepe tiene el pelo rubio, y lleva/tiene gafas, es competitivo, tiene 15 años y su cumpleaños es el 25 de enero. **[1 mark for each correct verb.]** [5]
3. **a)** trabaja – she works [1]
   b) viven – they live [1]
   c) Toco – I play [1]
   d) nadamos – we swim [1]

Page 110

1. **a)** Empiezo [1]
   b) piensa [1]
   c) cuesta [1]
   d) juegan, juego [2]
   e) llueve [1]
2. **a)** What is the weather like? [**tiempo** means time and weather] [1]
   b) It is cold. [Use **hacer** and not **ser** to describe weather.] [1]
   c) What do you do after school? [1]
   d) I always do my homework / prep. [1]
   e) I go horse riding on Saturday. [You can't say **Voy a la equitación** in Spanish, use the verb **hacer**.] [1]

3. a) empieza [1]
  b) hace frío [1]
  c) jugamos [1]
  d) hago [1]
  e) pensamos [1]
  f) vuelvo [1]
4. a) ir [1]
  b) van [1]
  c) voy [1]
  d) va [1]
  e) ver [1]

Page 111
1. a) I never go to the supermarket. [1]
  b) I don't see anyone in the park. [1]
  c) I don't do water sports. [1]
  d) I didn't do anything yesterday. [1]
2. a) Me gustan – plural needed [1]
  b) le gusta – he likes [1]
  c) Me encanta [1]
  d) me molesta – he annoys me, third person [1]
  e) me duele – singular needed [1]
  f) me gusta [1]
3. a) comí [1]
  b) jugué [1]
  c) toqué [1]
4. a) costaron [1]
  b) Tuviste [1]
  c) hizo [1]
  d) fui [1]

Page 112
1. iré, empezaré, tendré, haré, será [5]
2. ¡Hola!, ¿qué desea?
  Quiero comprar unos pantalones.
  ¿De qué color?
  Los quiero en gris.
  No los tengo en gris, sino en negro y azul marino.
  Vale, me gustan estos en negro, ¿puedo probarlos? or ¿los puedo probar?
  Sí, el probador está enfrente…

  5 minutos más tarde…
  ¡Me quedan muy bien! Quiero llevarlos or los quiero llevar.
  ¿Algo más?
  Sí, necesito un cinturón marrón.
  Aquí lo tiene en marrón.
  Lo llevo también.
  Vale, son 47 euros en total… [5]
3. I am called – me llamo; I wake up – me despierto; I get up – me levanto; I shower – me ducho; I get dressed – me visto; I have fun – me divierto; I go to bed – me acuesto [7]

Page 113
1. a) bebía, bebo [1]
  b) aprendía, aprendo [1]
2. a) C / PR, b) P, c) I, d) I / P [4]
3. a) haría: I would do [1]
  b) viajaría: I would travel [1]
  c) saldría: I would leave / go out [1]

> **Pages 114–127 Mixed Test-Style Questions**

1. a) puedo [1]
  b) puedes / se puede [1]
  c) puedo hacer [1]
  d) puedo visitar [1]
  e) hay [1]
  f) había [1]
  g) hay gente / personas [1]
  h) había contaminación / polución [1]

2. a) los gatos [1]
  b) los lápices [1]
  c) los centros comerciales [1]
  d) las catedrales [1]
  e) los peces [1]
  f) los profesores de ciencias [1]
3. a) Laura [1]
  b) Antonia [1]
  c) Antonia [1]
  d) Laura [1]
  e) Laura [1]
4. a) Hola, no puedo / no es posible mañana, pero el domingo, sí puedo [2]
  b) Me encantaría, ¿a qué hora? [1]
  c) Perfecto, ¿te apetece ir a la pizzería después de la película? [1]
5. a) True [1]
  b) False [1]
  c) True [1]
  d) True [1]
  e) False [1]
  f) False [1]
6. Mi pueblo es muy animado y —— hay mucho que hacer. [1]
  Mi pueblo es muy aislado —— y tranquilo. [1]
  El aire está muy contaminado —— a causa de los atascos. [1]
  Hay muchas flores y arboles —— en el jardín botánico. [1]
  Hay demasiada gente y —— está concurrido. [1]
  No hay suficientes —— tiendas. [1]
  Hay un mercado donde se puede —— comprar fruta y verduras. [1]
  Las instalaciones deportiva son —— estupendas. [1]
7. a) Selina [1]
  b) Marisa [1]
  c) Jaime [1]
  d) Selina [1]
  e) Selina [1]
  f) Marisa [1]
8. a) tengo [1]
  b) empiezo [1]
  c) son [1]
  d) gano [1]
  e) comprar [1]
9. No voy a hablar; —— tengo dolor de garganta. [1]
  Voy a ir al dentista; —— me duelen los dientes. [1]
  Quiero unas aspirinas; —— me duele la cabeza. [1]
  No puedo comer; —— tengo dolor de estómago. [1]
  No puedo hacer mis deberes; —— me duele la mano. [1]
  No quiero ir de paseo; —— me duelen los pies. [1]
10. a) end of June (this year) [1]
  b) no hot water, very small room [1]
  c) elderly dad, they were on fifth floor [1]
  d) 50% refund [1]
11. a) Me gustaría reservar una habitación doble para julio. [1]
  b) Desde el tres hasta el once de julio (desde… hace – from… until) [1]
  c) Para tres personas, dos adultos y un niño [1]
  d) ¿Cuánto es / cuánto cuesta / cuál es el precio? [1]
  e) ¿El desayuno está incluido? [1]
  f) ¡Perfecto! [1]
12. Trabajo [1] como médico [1] porque [1] me gusta ayudar [1] a otros. [1]
13. a) Voy al instituto.   1
  b) Voy a aprobar mis exámenes de GCSE.   2
  c) Voy a dejar el colegio.   3
  d) Voy a buscar un trabajo.   5
  e) Voy a ir a la universidad.   4
14. d), c), b), e), f), a)
15. a) True [
  b) False [
  c) True [
  d) False [

16. **a)** tengo [1]
    b) escuchar [1]
    c) clásica [1]
    d) compositor [1]
    e) el piano [1]
    f) prefiere [1]
    g) irá [1]
17. I live in a big, modern house [1]
    with my family. [1]
    I have two sisters and a brother. [1]
    My brother is [1]
    short but intelligent. [1]
    My sisters are fun [1]
    but sometimes [1]
    they get on my nerves. [1]
    I am athletic and I play volleyball [1]
    every Monday afternoon. [1]
18. **a)** mando / mandé mensajes [2]
    b) busco / busqué información [2]
    c) comparto / compartí fotos [2]
    d) hago / hice la compra en línea [2]
19. **a)** basketball [Could also be pelota '…para adultos'] [1]
    b) swimming [1]
    c) younger than 18. [1]
    d) dance shoes [1]
20. **a)** ciudad universitaria [1]
    b) mejorar [1]
    c) zonas peatonales [1]
    d) habrá [1]
21. **a)** Me llevo bien con mi familia. [2]
    b) Me gusta ver las películas de ciencia ficción. [2]
    c) Fuimos al cine el viernes pasado. [2]
    d) Mi hermano es muy inteligente y divertido. [2]
    [2 marks for each correct sentence, 1 mark for a partially correct sentence.]
22. un helado de —— vainilla / chocolate [1]
    un té —— con limón [1]
    un pastel de —— albaricoque [Could also be 'chocolate / vainilla'] [1]
    un sándwich —— de jamón [1]
    una tarta —— de café [1]
    un café con —— leche [1]
    un mousse de —— chocolate [1]
    la sopa de —— pescado [1]
23. **a)** muchas [1]
    b) mucho [1]
    c) mucha [1]
    d) muy, mucha [2]
    e) mucho, muy [2]
24. En este momento va **al colegio** y en junio va a aprobar los **exámenes**. Él va a **ir** a la **universidad** para **estudiar** ciencias. Quisiera **ser** médico. [6]
25. **a)** Firefighter / fireman [1]
    b) Footballer, well paid and exciting [1]
26. Jim – Fui a la playa con amigos, fui por una semana, fui en coche, me quedé en un albergue juvenil, tomé el sol.
    [1 mark for each correct verb.] [5]
    Gustavo – Fui a Roma solo, fui por un mes, fui en tren, me quedé en la casa de un amigo, aprendí el italiano.
    [1 mark for each correct verb.] [5]
27. **a)** Marta: 15 July [1]
    b) Sara: 17 November [1]
    c) Antonio: 1 February [1]
    d) José: 31 January [1]
    e) Ana: 25 March [1]
28. **a)** sailing [1]
    b) after school [1]
    c) at his grandma's house [1]
29. Recibo 10 —— libras cada mes. [1]
    El año pasado —— visité España. [1]

En dos meses —— iré a la universidad. [1]
Es importante —— ayudar en casa. [1]
Debería pasear —— a mi perro. [1]
Gasto mi dinero en —— revistas y maquillaje. [1]
30. **a)** Tengo doce años. [2]
    b) Mi cumpleaños es el veinticinco de septiembre. [2]
    c) Me gusta el chocolate, pero no me gustan los exámenes. [2]
    d) La iglesia es pequeña. [2]
31. **a)** Tengo [1]
    b) vivía [1]
    c) era [1]
    d) había [1]
    e) estaban [1]
    f) quedaba [1]
    g) hacía [1]
    h) vivo [1]
32. **a)** Mi colegio se llama… [1]
    b) Mi colegio se halla… / Mi colegio está… [1]
    c) En mi colegio hay… alumnos. [1]
    d) Las clases empiezan a las… [1]
    e) Durante la hora de comer juego al fútbol / como en la cantina / charlo con mis amigos. [Or any suitable activity in the present tense.] [1]
    f) Mi uniforme es… / Llevo unos pantalones negros y una camisa blanca con una chaqueta gris. [Or any other items of school uniform.] [1]
    g) Mi asignatura preferida es… [1]
    h) Las clases terminan a las… [1]
33. **a)** hago [1]
    b) hice [1]
    c) fui [1]
    d) voy a ir [1]
    e) tengo [1]
    f) voy a tener [1]
    g) tendría [1]
34. una camiseta —— T-shirt [1]
    una sudadera —— sweatshirt [1]
    una corbata —— tie [1]
    un vestido —— dress [1]
    un abrigo —— coat [1]
    unos zapatos —— shoes [1]
35. I live in a small town [1]
    in the north of Colombia. [1]
    My house is next to the park. [1]
    On Saturdays I like to ride my bike [1]
    with my friends. [1]
    Recently, I swam [1]
    in the swimming pool with my sister. [1]
    In the future I would like [1]
    to live in the south of Spain in Málaga [1]
    because there is always lots to do. [1]
36. **a)** typical food (of the region). [1]
    b) first right. [1]
    c) police station. [1]
    d) the USA. [1]
    e) heat / hot weather. [1]
37. **a)** diez [1]
    b) tres [1]
    c) comparto [1]
    d) genial [1]
    e) un televisor [1]
38. **a)** la piscina / el mar [1]
    b) el estadio [1]
    c) el museo [1]
    d) el parque / el jardín botánico [1]
39. Possible answer: Me gusta mucho ver los dibujos animados porque creo que son graciosos. [4]
40. **a)** negative [1]
    b) positive [1]
    c) negative [1]

d) positive [1]
e) positive [1]
f) negative [1]
g) positive [1]
h) negative [1]
41. c), f), a), b), g), e), d) [7]
42. Siempre voy a Grecia porque hace calor. [1]
43. Possible answers, any three [answers without 'puedo' also acceptable]:

Puedo hacer cursos en casa.	I can do courses at home.
Puedo contactar con personas en otros países fácilmente.	I can contact people in different countries easily.
Puedo estar en contacto con mis amigos.	I can be in contact with my friends.
Puedo estar al día de las noticias.	I can keep up to date with the news.
Puedo grabar momentos especiales.	I can record special moments.
Puedo jugar a los videojuegos.	I can play video games.
Puedo descargar música.	I can download music.
Puedo hacer compras en línea.	I can do online shopping.
Puedo organizar salidas con mis amigos.	I can arrange to go out with my friends.

[3]

44. Me apasiona el fútbol, es mi deporte favorito. Juego al fútbol a diario. [1]
Además, me mola el tenis y lo juego con mi hermano dos o tres veces por semana. [1]
Me gusta mucho la equitación, pero prefiero el tenis. [1]
No me gusta nada el rugby porque me aburre muchísimo. [1]
No soporto la natación porque odio mojarme. [1]

45. Siempre veo la tele con mis padres el domingo. Me encantan los documentales, pero a mi padre le gustan las noticias.
[1 mark for each correct verb.] [3]

46. **a)** español(a) [1]
b) inglés / inglesa [1]
c) francés / francesa [1]
d) alemán / alemana [1]

47. **a)** Gales [1]
b) Escocia [1]
c) Italia [1]
d) los Estados Unidos [1]

48. **a)** La fruta y las legumbres son *buenas* para la salud. [1]
b) Desayuno *café/cereales* con leche. [1]
c) Mi *fruta* preferida es una manzana. [1]
d) Hay que *comer* mucha ensalada. [1]
e) No hay que *fumar* muchos cigarrillos. [1]

Glossary

Family

a, *prep*, at / to
alto, *adj*, tal
aniversario, *nm*, birthday
bajo, *adj*, short
conejo, *nm*, rabbit
delgado, *adj*, slim
español, *adj*, Spanish
familia, *nf*, family
gato, *nm*, cat
gemelo, *adj*, twin
gordo, *adj*, fat
hermanastra, *nf*, step- or half-sister
hermanastro, *nm*, step- or half-brother
hija, *nf*, daughter
hijo, *nm*, son
hija única, *nf*, only child
hijo único, *nm*, only child
inglés, *adj*, English
liso, *adj*, straight
ojos, *nmpl*, eyes
pájaro, *nm*, bird
pelirrojo, *adj*, ginger
pelo, *nm*, hair
perezoso, *adj*, lazy
perro, *nm*, dog
pez, *nm*, fish
ratón, *nm*, mouse
rizado, *adj*, curly
tío / tía, *nm / nf*, uncle / aunt

House and Home

apartamento, *nm*, flat / apartment
armario, *nm*, wardrobe

aseo, *nm*, toilet
cama, *nf*, bed
campo, *nm*, countryside
casa, *nf*, house
cerca de, *prep*, near
ciudad, *nf*, city
cocina, *nf*, kitchen
comedor, *nm*, dining room
compartir, *vb*, to share
cuarto de baño, *nm*, bathroom
delante de, *prep*, in front of
detrás de, *prep*, behind
donde, *adv*, where
dormitorio, *nm*, bedroom
en, *prep*, in / on
España, *nf*, Spain
este, *nm*, east
habitación, *nf*, (bed)room
Inglaterra, *nf*, England
jardín, *nm*, garden
lado del mar, *nm*, seaside
lejos de, *prep*, far
norte, *nm*, north
oeste, *nm*, west
pueblo, *nm*, town
Reino Unido, *nm*, United Kingdom
salón, *nm*, living room
silla, *nf*, chair
sobre, *prep*, on / above
sur, *nm*, south

Food and Drink

agua mineral, *nm*, mineral water
a menudo, *adv*, often
a veces, *adv*, sometimes

beber, *vb*, to drink
bocadillo de jamón, *nm*, ham sandwich
bocadillo de queso, *nm*, cheese sandwich
café con leche, *nm*, coffee with milk
cebolla, *nf*, onion
champiñón, *nm*, mushroom
chocolate caliente, *nm*, hot chocolate
coca cola, *nf*, coca cola
coliflor, *nm*, cauliflower
comer, *vb*, to eat
de vez en cuando, *adv*, now and then
fresa, *nf*, strawberry
fruta, *nf*, fruit
guisante, *nm*, pea
helado, *nm*, ice cream
limón, *nm*, lemon
limonada, *nf*, lemonade
manzana, *nf*, apple
mariscos, *nmpl*, seafood / shellfish
melocotón, *nm*, peach
patata, *nf*, potato
pera, *nf*, pear
pescado, *nm*, fish
plátano, *nm*, banana
pollo, *nm*, chicken
rara vez, *adv*, rarely
todos los días, *adv*, every day
tortilla española, *nf*, Spanish omelette
verduras, *nfpl*, vegetables
zanahoria, *nf*, carrot
zumo de naranja, *nm*, orange juice

Sport and Health

ajedrez, *nm*, chess
bádminton, *nm*, badminton
baloncesto, *nm*, basketball
brazo, *nm*, arm
cabeza, *nf*, head
ciclismo, *nm*, cycling
cita, *nf*, appointment
dentista, *nm/f*, dentist
dientes, *nfpl*, teeth
enfermo, *adj*, ill
equitación, *nf*, horse-riding
espalda, *nf*, back
esquí, *nm*, skiing
estómago, *nm*, stomach
farmacia, *nf*, pharmacy
fútbol, *nm*, football
fumar, *vb*, to smoke
garganta, *nf*, throat
gripe, *nf*, flu
hacer, *vb*, to do
hospital, *nm*, hospital
juegos de mesa, *nmpl*, board games
jugar, *vb* to play
médico, *nm*, doctor
mini-golf, *nm*, mini-golf
natación, *nf*, swimming
ojos, *nmpl*, eyes
orejas, *nfpl*, ears
patinaje, *nm*, skating
pelota, *nf*, ball / Spanish handball
pie, *nm*, foot
pierna, *nf*, leg
rugby, *nm*, rugby
tenis, *nm*, tennis
tenis de mesa, *nm*, table tennis
tos, *nf*, cough

School and Education

aburrido, *adj*, boring
alemán, *nm*, German
alumno, *nm*, student / pupil
biblioteca, *nf*, library
biología, *nf*, biology
cantina, *nf*, canteen
chungo, *adj*, rubbish
ciencias, *nfpl*, science
clase, *nf*, class / lesson
dibujo, *nm*, art
difícil, *adj*, difficult
divertido, *adj*, fun
duro, *adj*, hard
edificio, *nm*, building
educación física, *nf*, PE
empezar, *vb*, to start
español, *nm*, Spanish
fácil, *adj*, easy
física, *nf*, physics
francés, *nm*, French
genial, *adj*, great
geografía, *nf*, geography
historia, *nf*, history
hora de comer, *nf*, lunch break
informática, *nf*, ICT
inglés, *nm*, English
interesante, *adj*, interesting
inútil, *adj*, useless
matemáticas, *nfpl*, maths
música, *nf*, music
patio, *nm*, yard
profesor(a), *nm(f)*, teacher
química, *nf*, chemistry
recreo, *nm*, break
religión, *nf*, RE
terminar, *vb*, to finish
tecnología, *nf*, technology

uniforme escolar, *nm*, school uniform
útil, *adj*, useful

Future Plans

abogado(a), *nm(f)*, lawyer
bien pagado, *adj*, well paid
cantante, *nm/f*, singer
comunicar, *vb*, to communicate
cooperar, *vb*, to co-operate
cortés, *adj*, courteous
creer, *vb*, to believe
dinámico, *adj*, energetic
director(a) de tienda, *nm(f)*, shop manager
diseñador(a) de videojuegos, *nm(f)*, video game designer
enfermero(a), *nm(f)*, nurse
estudiar, *vb*, to study
futbolista, *nm/f*, footballer
ganar, *vb*, to earn/win
gratificante, *adj*, rewarding
ingeniero(a), *nm(f)*, engineer
médico(a), *nm(f)*, doctor
organizado, *adj*, organised
paciente, *adj*, patient
peluquero(a), *nm(f)*, hairdresser
periodista, *nm/f*, journalist
piloto(a), *nm(f)*, pilot
profesor(a), *nm(f)*, teacher
respetuoso, *adj*, respectful
trabajador(a), *adj*, hard-working
trabajar, *vb*, to work
veterinario(a), *nm(f)*, vet

Leisure

batería, *nf*, drums
comedia, *nf*, comedy

concierto, *nm*, concert
detestar, *vb*, to detest
dibujo animado, *nm*, cartoon
entretenido, *adj*, entertaining
escuchar, *vb*, to listen
flauta, *nf*, flute
grupo, *nf*, band / group
guitarra, *nf*, guitar
gustar, *vb*, to like
ir, *vb*, to go
música clásica / rock, *nf*, classical / rock music
odiar, *vb*, to hate
película de acción, *nf*, action film
película de aventura, *nf*, adventure film
película de ciencia ficción, *nf*, science fiction film
película de terror, *nf*, horror film
película histórica, *nf*, historical film
película romántica, *nf*, romantic film
piscina, *nf*, swimming pool
pista de patinaje, *nf*, ice rink
polideportivo, *nm*, leisure / sports centre
preferido, *adj*, preferred / favourite
preferir, *vb*, to prefer
relajante, *adj*, relaxing
tocar + instrumento, *vb*, to play (an instrument)
vamos, *vb*, we go
voy, *vb*, I go
violín, *nm*, violin

TV and Technology

aterrador, *adj*, scary
bastante, *adv*, quite / enough
chatear, *vb*, to chat online
descargar, *vb*, to download
demasiado, *adv*, too much
concurso, *nm*, quiz show
de miedo, *adj*, scary
documental, *nm*, documentary
educativo, *adj*, educational
emocional, *adj*, emotional
emocionante, *adj*, exciting
fin de semana, *nm*, weekend
mandar, *vb*, to send
muy, *adv*, very
no…, *adv*, no / not
no…más, *adv*, no longer
no…nunca, *adv*, never
noticias, *nfpl*, news
película, *nf*, film
poco, *adv*, few / little;
un poco, *adj*, a little bit
programa de telerrealidad, *nm*, reality TV programme
raramente, *adv*, rarely
series, *nfpl*, series
telenovela, *nf*, soap opera
tiempo, *nm*, weather, time
ver, *vb*, to watch
verdaderamente, *adv*, really / truly

Shopping and Money

abrigo, *nm*, overcoat
ahorrar, *vb*, to save
calcetines, *nmpl*, socks
camisa, *nf*, shirt
camiseta, *nf*, T-shirt

chándal, *nm*, tracksuit
chaqueta, *nf*, jacket
chulo, *adj*, cool
comprar, *vb*, to buy
corbata, *nf*, tie
cuidar, *vb*, to look after
de moda, *adj*, fashionable / trendy
de rayas, *adj*, striped
falda, *nf*, skirt
feo, *adj*, ugly
fuera de moda, *adj*, old fashioned
gafas, *nfpl*, glasses
hacer de canguro, *vb*, to babysit
jersey, *nm*, jumper
medias, *nf*, tights
pantalones, *nmpl*, trousers
recibir, *vb*, to receive
sombrero, *nm*, hat
sudadera con capuche, *nf*, hoodie
trabajo a tiempo parcial, *nm*, part-time job
vaqueros, *nmpl*, jeans
vestido, *nm*, dress
zapatillas de deporte, *nfpl*, trainers
zapatos, *nmpl*, shoes

Where I Live

afueras, *nfpl*, suburbs
animado, *adj*, lively
ayuntamiento, *nm*, town hall
centro comercial, *nm*, shopping centre
centro de la ciudad, *nm*, city centre
centro de ocio, *nm*, leisure centre

construir, *vb*, to construct / build

continuar, *vb*, to continue

crear, *vb*, to create

estación, *nf*, station

girar, *vb*, to turn

iglesia, *nf*, church

mercado, *nm*, market

mucho, *adv*, a lot of / many

polución, *nf*, pollution

pueblecito, *nm*, village

ruidoso, *adj*, noisy

sucio, *adj*, dirty

tienda, *nf*, shop

tomar, *vb*, to take

tranquilo, *adj*, quiet

vivir, *vb*, to live

zona peatonal, *nf*, pedestrianised zone

Holidays

a, *prep*, to

albergue juvenil, *nm*, youth hostel

avión, *nm*, plane

balcón, *nm*, balcony

camping, *nm*, campsite

caravana, *nf*, caravan

coche, *nm*, car

con, *prep*, with

ducha, *nf*, shower

en, *prep*, by +means of transport

los Estados Unidos, *nmpl*, United States

Gran Bretaña, *nf*, Great Britain

hacer compras, *vb*, to shop

montaña, *nf*, mountain

noche, *nf*, night

país, *nm*, country

playa, *nf*, beach

quedarse, *vb*, to stay

roto, *adj*, broken

ruido, *adj*, noise

sin, *prep*, without

tienda de campaña, *nf*, tent

vacaciones, *nfpl*, holiday(s)

viajar, *vb*, to travel

visitar, *vb*, to visit

Global Issues

apoyar, *vb*, to support

calentamiento global, *nm*, global warming

conservar, *vb*, to conserve

crueldad, *nf*, cruelty

deforestación, *nf*, deforestation

energía, *nf*, energy

evitar, *vb*, to avoid

guerra, *nf*, war

hambre, *nm*, hunger

intentar, *vb*, to try

luchar, *vb*, to fight

más, *adv*, more

menos, *adv*, less

pensar, *vb*, to think

pobreza, *nf*, poverty

proteger, *vb*, to protect

reciclaje, *nm*, recycling

reciclar, *vb*, to recycle

respetar, *vb*, to respect

salvar, *vb*, to save

suficiente, *adv*, enough

tanto, *adv*, so much / so many

terrorismo, *nm*, terrorism

tirar, *vb*, to throw (away)

Index

Collins

KS3
Spanish
Workbook

with audio download

Helen Farrar and Sherrie A Spinks

Revision Tips

Rethink Revision

Have you ever taken part in a quiz and thought *'I know this!'*, but no matter how hard you scrabbled around in your brain you just couldn't come up with the answer?

It's very frustrating when this happens, but in a fun situation it doesn't really matter. However, in tests and assessments, it is essential that you can recall the relevant information when you need to.

Most students think that revision is about making sure you **know** *stuff*, but it is also about being confident that you can **retain** that *stuff* over time and **recall** it when needed.

Revision that Really Works

Experts have found that there are two techniques that help with *all* of these things and consistently produce better results in tests and exams compared to other revision techniques.

Applying these techniques to your KS3 revision will ensure you get better results in tests and assessments and will have all the relevant knowledge at your fingertips when you start studying for your GCSEs.

It really isn't rocket science either – you simply need to:
- **test yourself** on each topic as many times as possible
- **leave a gap** between the test sessions.

It is most effective if you leave a good period of time between the test sessions, e.g. between a week and a month. The idea is that just as you start to forget the information, you force yourself to recall it again, keeping it fresh in your mind.

Three Essential Revision Tips

1 Use Your Time Wisely
- Allow yourself plenty of time
- Try to start revising six months before tests and assessments – it's more effective and less stressful
- Your revision time is precious so use it wisely – using the techniques described on this page will ensure you revise effectively and efficiently and get the best results
- Don't waste time re-reading the same information over and over again – it's time-consuming and not effective!

2 Make a Plan
- Identify all the topics you need to revise (this Complete Revision & Practice book will help you)
- Plan at least five sessions for each topic
- A one-hour session should be ample to test yourself on the key ideas for a topic
- Spread out the practice sessions for each topic – the optimum time to leave between each session is about one month but, if this isn't possible, just make the gaps as big as realistically possible.

3 Test Yourself
- Methods for testing yourself include: quizzes, practice questions, flashcards, past-papers, explaining a topic to someone else, etc.
- This Complete Revision & Practice book gives you seven practice test opportunities per topic
- Don't worry if you get an answer wrong – provided you check what the right answer is, you are more likely to get the same or similar questions right in future!

Visit our website to download your free flashcards, for more information about the benefits of these revision techniques and for further guidance on how to plan ahead and make them work for you.

collins.co.uk/collinsks3revision

Contents

Family and Home

Family

1 The box below shows people's birthdays. Match the statements below to the correct person.

Juan: 1 / 6 / 98	Carla: 6 / 4 / 02	Sara: 17 / 11 / 01	Marta: 15 / 8 / 00
Miguel: 21 / 10 / 95	Alejandro: 31 / 5 / 96	Felipe: 11 / 7 / 99	Ana: 24 / 9 / 97

a) **Mi cumpleaños es el once de julio.** ....

b) **Mi cumpleaños es el primero de junio.** ....

c) **Mi cumpleaños es el veintiuno de octubre.** ....

d) **Mi cumpleaños es el treinta y uno de mayo.** ....

e) **Mi cumpleaños es el quince de agosto.** .... **[5]**

2 Write out the birthdays of the remaining three people in question 1.

a) **Mi cumpleaños es el** ....

b) **Mi cumpleaños es el** ....

c) **Mi cumpleaños es el** .... **[3]**

3 Read the descriptions below and then answer the questions that follow.

Marina López, atleta: Tengo el pelo largo y castaño y los ojos verdes.

Aurelia Cruz, esquiadora: Soy bastante alta. Mido 1m 67cm. Tengo el pelo rubio y los ojos castaños.

Sergio Hernández, jugador de rugby: Soy muy alto y tengo el pelo muy corto y rizado.

Paulina Mayol, nadadora: Tengo los ojos azules y el pelo ni corto ni largo.

a) Who has long hair? ....

b) Who is very tall? ....

c) Who has brown eyes? .... **[3]**

4 Translate the descriptions below into English.

a) **Tengo el pelo castaño, largo y liso. Tengo los ojos azules y soy muy alta.**

....

.... **[6]**

b) Soy bastante bajo y tengo los ojos marrones. Tengo el pelo negro y corto.

_____

_____ [5]

c) Somos gemelos. Tenemos el pelo pelirrojo, rizado y muy largo.

_____

_____ [6]

d) Tengo un gato blanco y pequeño.

_____ [3]

5 Read what Miguel, Lucía and Enrique have to say about themselves, then answer the questions below.

Miguel:

¡Hola! Me llamo Miguel y vivo en la República Dominicana; es una isla en el Caribe. Hablo español y francés. Tengo una familia numerosa: tengo dos hermanas y tres hermanos y vivo con mis padres. Mi cumpleaños es el seis de mayo, pues tengo casi catorce años.

Lucía:

¡Buenos días! Me llamo Lucía y vivo en Santiago, Chile, con mi madre. Mi cumpleaños es el siete de julio. Tengo catorce años. Mis padres están divorciados. Tengo un hermanastro que se llama Andrés. Todavía es un bebé; él tiene un año.

Enrique:

¡Hola! Me llamo Enrique y soy argentino. Hablo español e inglés. Vivo con mis padres y mis dos hermanos. Mis hermanos son gemelos y tienen nueve años. Mi madre se llama Marisa y tiene cuarenta años. Mi padre, que se llama Pedro; tiene cuarenta y tres años.

What do the numbers below represent?

a) 6 is _____

b) 13 is _____

c) 40 is _____

d) 43 is _____

e) 14 is _____ [5]

Total Marks _____ / 36

Family and Home

House and Home

1 Rearrange the words below to make Spanish sentences and then translate them into English.

a) en sur el vivo España de

_____

_____

b) casa se halla mi el en de la ciudad centro

_____

_____

c) habitaciones hay nueve nuestra casa en

_____

_____

d) tenemos no jardín

_____

_____

e) casa nuestra tiene plantas dos un y ático

_____

_____

f) la hay planta dormitorios primera tres en

_____

_____

g) habitación está de al mis de padres mi lado dormitorio la

_____

_____

h) dormitorio pero bonito muy pequeño mi es

_____

_____

i) dormitorio muchas en hay mi cosas

....

....

j) en dormitorio televisor mi tengo no

....

.... [20]

2 Insert **mi** or **mis** into the sentences below.

a) .... casa es muy grande.

b) En .... dormitorio hay un ordenador.

c) .... libros están en .... estantería.

d) El dormitorio de .... padres está al lado de .... dormitorio.

e) .... ciudad está en el centro de España.

f) .... primos viven en Murcia.

g) .... abuela vive con nosotros.

h) .... jardín es muy pequeño. [10]

3 Draw a line to match the questions and answers.

¿Dónde vives?	Sí, porque mis amigos viven aquí también.
¿Vives lejos de la costa?	Sí, paso la aspiradora a menudo.
¿Te gusta tu ciudad?	No, pero tenemos un portátil en el salón.
¿Cómo es tu casa?	No, bastante cerca; está a unos diez minutos.
¿Tienes jardín?	Hay mi cama y mi armario.
¿Ayudas a tus padres en casa?	Es bastante pequeña.
¿Qué hay en tu dormitorio?	Sí, y es muy grande.
¿Tienes un ordenador en tu dormitorio?	Vivo en Alicante, cerca de la costa.

[8]

Total Marks .... / 38

Lifestyle

Food and Drink

1 Look at the images below and then make a note of each correct price.

a) **pescado** ....

b) **zumo de manzana** ....

c) **naranjas** ....

d) **agua mineral** ....

e) **bocadillo de jamón** ....

f) **leche** ....   **[6]**

2 Read the menu from a Spanish restaurant and choose an appropriate dish for the following people.

a) Paula is vegetarian, but she eats eggs.

....

b) Verónica would like a sandwich but she does not eat fish.

....

c) Álvaro has a sweet tooth.

....

Bocadillo de queso	**Calamares**
Sopa de tomate	**Albóndigas**
Tortilla Española	**Tarta de limón**
Bocadillo de jamón	**Sándwich de atún**
Pollo asado con patatas fritas	

d) Laura is not very hungry, so she would like some soup.

_____

e) Arturo would like some seafood.

_____   [5]

3 Read the following text and fill in the blanks with the words provided in the box.

espaguetis   leche   limonada   naranja   italiana   pizza

Yo prefiero la cocina _____ porque me encanta la pasta y los

_____. Me mola la _____ de champiñones. De postre

me chiflan los helados. Normalmente bebo un zumo de _____ porque

no soporto las bebidas gaseosas, como la _____. De vez en cuando

tomo una bebida caliente como el café con _____, por ejemplo.   [6]

4 Read the following statements. What opinion is given about food and drink?

Write P for a positive opinion.

Write N for a negative opinion.

Write P / N for a positive and a negative opinion.

a) Como manzanas porque me gusta el sabor.   _____

b) Tomo cinco raciones de fruta y verduras
cada día porque es bueno para la salud.   _____

c) No como guisantes porque no me gustan las legumbres.   _____

d) Me chifla el queso, pero es malo para la salud.   _____

e) Me mola beber té cada día.   _____

f) De vez en cuando como pescado, pero es caro.   _____

g) Las galletas son demasiado dulces.   _____   [7]

Total Marks _____ / 24

Lifestyle

Sport and Health

1 Link the following sentences together.

El fin de semana me gusta ir a la piscina	como la vela.
El fin de semana me mola hacer equitación	porque me chiflan los caballos.
A menudo monto en bicicleta	donde hago natación.
Me encantan los deportes acuáticos	porque me flipa el ciclismo.
Me gusta ver partidos de fútbol,	pero me caigo a menudo.
Adoro el patinaje	voy con frecuencia al estadio.

[6]

2 Read the following information about different sports.

Write P for a positive opinion.

Write N for a negative opinion.

Write P / N for a positive and a negative opinion.

a) El hockey no me gusta nada porque me parece demasiado aburrido. ....

b) Voy a la piscina a menudo con mis amigos sin embargo es bastante caro. ....

c) A mi amigo le encanta el esquí acuático, pero para mí es un deporte
peligroso. ....

d) Me chifla el fútbol. Me parece interesante y emocionante. ....

e) La gimnasia me hace bien, pero me parece agotadora. ....

f) Encuentro el tenis increíble. Mi tenista favorito es Rafael Nadal. ....

g) Por otro lado, la pelota no me interesa. Es monótona. ....

h) Recomiendo los deportes de invierno. El año pasado hice esquí en la
Sierra Nevada con mi familia y fue fantástico. .... [8]

3 The people below are describing how they stay healthy. Which picture is relevant to what each person is saying?

A   B   C   D

E   F   G

a) **Bebo un litro de agua mineral cada día.** ⸻

b) **Soy muy activo. Voy al gimnasio a diario.** ⸻

c) **No fumo nunca.** ⸻

d) **No bebo café sino el té verde.** ⸻

e) **Me acuesto temprano y duermo ocho horas por noche.** ⸻

f) **Nunca tomo galletas y tampoco pasteles.** ⸻

g) **Para evitar el estrés leo un libro.** ⸻   [7]

4 Fill in the blanks in each sentence below by choosing the correct word from the box.

| malo | bueno | forma | deportista | verduras |
| cáncer | natación | equitación | violento | |

a) **Soy muy** ⸻**. Juego al tenis, al fútbol y voy al gimnasio.**

b) **Odio el rugby porque me parece aburrido y demasiado** ⸻**.**

c) **El fin de semana pasado, fui a la piscina donde hice la** ⸻

d) **No fumo nunca porque es** ⸻ **para la salud y causa**

⸻**.**

e) **Para mantenerme en** ⸻**, como mucha fruta y muchas**

⸻**.**   [7]

Total Marks ⸻ / 28

Education and Future Plans

School and Education

1 Match the images to the sentences below. Be careful as only six images are used!

A    B   C   D

E    F   G

a) Voy a aprobar el bachillerato porque me gustaría estudiar ciencias. ....

b) Me mola el inglés, pero el profe es muy antipático. ....

c) Me encanta el deporte a pesar del profe. ....

d) Voy a trabajar muy duro sobre todo en informática. ....

e) No soporto la geografía porque es aburrida. ....

f) Odio la historia. Soy muy débil en historia. ....   [6]

2 Choose the correct word to complete each sentence below.

a) No me gusta el inglés. Las clases me parecen ....

   aburridas   aburrido   interesantes

b) Me encanta ir al colegio pero tengo muchos ....

   clase   deberes   amigo

c) La historia no me gusta. Me parece ....

   interesante   aburrida   divertida

d) Me chifla mi colegio porque los profesores son ....

   antipáticos   aburridos   simpáticos

e) No soporto la química porque no soy .... en ciencias.

   débil   fuerte   súper

f) En la biblioteca no hay suficientes ....

   libros   gomas   cuadernos   [6]

3 Decide whether these school rules are true or false. Write **T** for true or **F** for false.

a) **No está permitido comer chicle en clase.** ....

b) **Está prohibido fumar en los aseos.** ....

c) **No se puede jugar al fútbol en la biblioteca.** ....

d) **Hay que enviar mensajes a los amigos en clase.** ....

e) **No se debe escribir grafiti en las paredes.** ....

f) **No hay que hacer los deberes.** ....   **[6]**

4 Read what Carmen, Arturo and Selina think about their schools.

Carmen	Arturo	Selina
Me gusta mucho mi colegio. Tengo muchos amigos y nos divertimos. Pero la cantina es demasiado pequeña y no tenemos bastantes ordenadores.	**Detesto el ambiente en mi colegio. Es demasiado estresante. Para los profesores solo los deberes son importantes. No puedo salir entresemana porque tengo demasiado trabajo escolar.**	**Siempre es muy difícil trabajar en clase porque muchos alumnos son perezosos y el comportamiento es terrible. Los estudiantes no trabajan y no escuchan a los profes.**

Who says the following?

a) I find school very stressful. ....

b) Other pupils misbehave. ....

c) I have fun with my friends. ....

d) I would like a larger canteen. ....

e) The teachers give too much work to the pupils. ....

f) I would like more computers in school. ....

g) I have so much work I can't go out in the week. ....

h) I find lots of pupils lazy. ....   **[8]**

Total Marks .... / 26

Education and Future Plans

Future Plans

1 Draw lines to match the Spanish time phrases with their English equivalents.

después	in three years
el año próximo	afterwards
luego	first of all
en el futuro	in the future
ante todo	next year
dentro de tres años	then / next

[6]

2 Write the feminine versions of these jobs.

Masculine   Feminine

a) **abogado** ....

b) **peluquero** ....

c) **director** ....

d) **enfermero** ....

e) **dentista** ....

[5]

3 Complete the sentences below with the correct infinitive from the box.

vivir	tener	viajar	continuar	dejar	ir

a) Voy a .... el colegio.

b) Voy a .... con mis estudios.

c) Voy a .... a la universidad.

d) Voy a .... al extranjero.

e) Voy a .... en una casa grande.

f) Voy a .... hijos.

[6]

4 Rearrange the words in Spanish so that they make sense. Then translate them into English.

a) **estar   necesito   motivado**

....

....

b) **cooperar   sus   tiene   con   que   compañeros**

....

....

c) **comunicar   ideas   puedo   mis**

....

.... **[6]**

5 Read what Ana says below and answer the questions in English.

> Me llamo Ana y soy traductora. Me gusta el trabajo porque me siento siempre motivada. Además, puedo trabajar sola o en equipo y entonces es muy variado. A la universidad, estudié inglés y francés pues yo puedo comunicar con muchas personas diferentes. Gozo de mi trabajo porque es muy interesante y bastante bien pagado. En el futuro quiero trabajar al extranjero ya que será gratificante y muy emocionante.

a) What is Ana's job? ....

b) Why does Ana say her job is varied? ....

c) What has studying English and French allowed her to do?

....

d) Why does she like her job?

....

e) What would she like to do in the future and why?

.... **[5]**

Total Marks .... **/ 28**

Leisure, Free Time and Media

1. Write the correct time and meeting place in English.

   Example: **Te veo delante del cine a las seis de la tarde.**

   6 pm, in front of the cinema

   a) **Quedamos en el centro comercial a las once de la mañana.**

   _____

   b) **Nos encontramos a las ocho y media de la tarde fuera de la bolera.**

   _____

   c) **Nos vemos mañana por la mañana a las nueve enfrente de la biblioteca.**

   _____ [3]

2. Match up the two halves of each sentence to complete the questions.

¿Te apetece ir a la	de atracciones el sábado?
¿Quieres comer después de	de rock mañana, ¿quieres venir?
¿Tienes ganas de pasear	bolera este viernes?
¿Quieres venir al parque	ver la película?
Tengo una entrada para el concierto	a mi perro conmigo?

   [5]

3. Write a text to your friend inviting them out. Include the following details:

   Where: the beach

   When: Sunday afternoon, 2 pm

   Meet: outside the café

   _____

   _____

   _____ [3]

4 For each photo, write a sentence to say you are going there and at the time stated.

Example: **Voy al teatro a las siete de la tarde.**

a) Swimming pool: 1 pm

_____

b) Library: 10 am

_____

c) Park: 11.30 am

_____

d) Shopping centre: 12 pm

_____ **[4]**

5 Fill in the gaps in this dialogue about arranging to go out using the words below. An extra word has been added to the box to make your choice more difficult!

cuándo	abuela	ir	posible	próximo	puedo

¡Hola Leticia!...¿Te apetece a) _____ *al concierto de jazz en el parque?*

b) ¿ _____ *es?*

Pues, el domingo c) _____

Lo siento, no d) _____

¿Por qué?

Tengo que visitar a mi e) _____

Pues, ¡qué lástima! **[5]**

Total Marks _____ **/ 20**

Leisure, Free Time and Media

 1 Write the Spanish below for each type of programme.

a)

b)

c)

....

d)

e)

f)

[6]

....

2 For each programme in question 1, write a sentence to give your opinion. Make sure they are plural! e.g.

a) Me encantan los dibujos animados porque son entretenidos.

b) ....

c) ....

d) ....

e) ....

f) .... **[10]**

3 Draw lines to match up the Spanish frequency words with their meanings.

De vez en cuando	never
Todos los días	rarely
Nunca	sometimes
Siempre	every day
A menudo	twice a week
Dos veces a la semana	always
Raramente	often

[7]

4 Improve this sentence by adding in a frequency word, a connective and an opinion.

Veo las emisiones de música.

.... **[3]**

5 Look at the text, which has been partially translated. Fill in the missing parts.

Hola me llamo Layla y I live with my mum **a)** ....

en el centro de Bogotá, un pueblo en Colombia. I love to watch soaps

b) .... **y mi favorita se llama 'Chica Vampiro'.**

La ponen en la tele three times a week **c)** .... ,

el lunes, Wednesday **d)** .... **y viernes. Mi**

madre piensa que paso too much time **e)** ....

viendo la tele, pero no agree **f)** ....

Ayer vi an English film **g)** ...., **creo que fue**

great **h)** .... ! **[8]**

6 Look at the translations about the advantages of technology and correct the error in each English sentence.

a) Se puede hacer cursos en casa.   You can do competitions at home.

....

b) Puedo estar en contacto con mis tíos.   I can be in touch with my cousins.

....

c) Puedo grabar momentos especiales.   I can see special moments.

....

d) Puedo buscar información.   I can find information.

....

e) Se puede organizar las entradas.   You can organise trips.

....

f) Me ayuda con los estudios.   It encourages me to do my studies.

.... **[6]**

Total Marks .... **/ 40**

Leisure, Free Time and Media

Shopping and Money

1 Reorder these sentences and then translate them into English.

a) unos   algodón   llevo   azules   de   pantalones

....

....

b) mis   gustan   zapatillas   blancas   me   mucho   deporte   de

....

....

c) llevar   colegio   prefiero   al   vaqueros   son   cómodos   porque

....

.... **[3]**

2 These Spanish translations each contain one error. Rewrite each sentence correctly.

a) a green and white T-shirt   **una verde y blanca camiseta**

....

b) a black fashionable jacket   **una chaqueta negra fuera de moda**

.... **[2]**

3 Put this shopping dialogue in the correct order. Start with the shop assistant.

a) ¿De qué color y qué número?

b) Quiero comprar unos zapatos elegantes.

c) ¿Cuánto son?

d) ¿Qué desea?

e) Aquí tiene.

f) Pues… creo que llevo el 37 y prefiero marrón.

g) ¡Qué barato! Me los llevo.

h) Hoy están de oferta, a solo 35 euros. .... **[8]**

4 Read what Ignacio says about pocket money and work and fill in the gaps below in English.

> Soy Ignacio y soy hijo único, por eso tengo que ayudar mucho en casa, por ejemplo, tengo que lavar los platos y pasear al perro. El fin de semana trabajo en el jardín, no me molesta y creo que es justo. Afortunadamente recibo 30 euros al mes y creo que es mucho. Siempre ahorro 10 euros y gasto 20 euros en revistas, caramelos y otras cosas. Tengo mucha suerte porque mis padres compran mi ropa.

a) Ignacio is an only.. .

b) He has to .... at the weekend.

c) He thinks it's ....

d) He thinks he gets .... pocket money.

e) He .... 10 euros a month.

f) His parents buy his .... [6]

5 Answer the following questions in Spanish about pocket money and work.

a) ¿Cuánto dinero de bolsillo recibes?

....

b) ¿Qué tareas en casa haces?

....

c) ¿En qué gastas tu dinero?

.... [3]

6 Draw lines to match up these jobs.

Reparto periódicos.	I help my parents.
Trabajo en una peluquería.	I work in a shop.
Hago de canguro.	I deliver newspapers.
Trabajo en una tienda.	I work in a hairdressers.
Ayudo a mis padres.	I do babysitting.

[5]

Total Marks .... / 27

The Wider World

1 The places in the box below are described in the sentences. Write the correct place for each sentence.

el mercado	la biblioteca	la iglesia	el estadio
el museo	el polideportivo	el jardín botánico / parque	

a) Puedo comprar verduras frescas, tiene lugar cada sábado en la plaza.

  _____

b) Hago muchas actividades aquí, por ejemplo, el baloncesto, el squash y el tenis de mesa.

  _____

c) Voy ahí para leer y para buscar información. _____

d) Voy cada domingo a las 10 de la mañana, es un lugar espiritual. _____

e) Mi equipo favorito juega ahí. _____

f) Puedo aprender mucho sobre la historia local, la entrada es gratis. _____

g) Se puede ver árboles muy viejos, ¡es muy pintoresco! _____ [7]

2 Write the question which best fits these answers on the topic of town.

a) _____

  Sí, me encanta vivir en mi pueblo porque es animado.

b) _____

  Mi abuela vive en el campo.

c) _____

  Prefiero vivir en la ciudad.

d) _____

  Brighton está en la costa.

e) _____

  Vivo con mi madre y mi hermano menor. [5]

3 Follow the directions and choose the letter that shows your destination. Your starting point is always at the bottom.

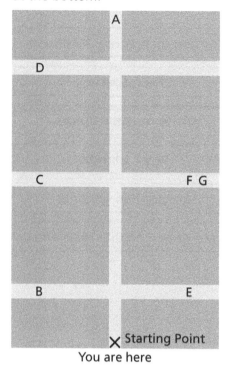

You are here

a) **Para ir a la piscina, toma la tercera calle a la izquierda.** ....

b) **Para ir a la biblioteca toma la segunda calle a la derecha, está al final de la calle.** ....

c) **Para ir al museo, sigue todo recto y está al final de la calle.** ....

d) **La catedral está al lado de la biblioteca.** ....

e) **Correos está al final de la primera calle a la izquierda.** ....

f) **Tienes que tomar la segunda calle a la izquierda para tomar el tren a Madrid.** ....

g) **Hay un buen restaurante al final de la primera calle a la derecha.** .... [7]

4 Read Francesca's description of her town and answer the questions in English.

Puerto Vallarta es un pueblo turístico que se encuentra en la costa este de México. Hay muchos hoteles de cinco estrellas, y restaurantes y bares a donde van los turistas. La mayoría viene de los Estados Unidos. Las playas son la atracción más importante y tienen arena muy fina y dorada. Los Arcos es el nombre de un grupo de islas con cuevas donde se puede bucear e incluso ver ballenas. Recomiendo una visita a mi pueblo porque tiene unas vistas preciosas, la gente local es muy amable y finalmente tiene un clima muy agradable.

a) Where is Puerto Vallarta situated? .... [1]

b) Where do the majority of tourists come from? .... [1]

c) How does she describe the beaches? .... [2]

d) What two things can you do at Los Arcos? .... [2]

e) Why should you visit Puerto Vallarta? .... [3]

....

Total Marks .... **/ 28**

The Wider World

Holidays

1 Draw lines to match the questions and answers.

¿Adónde vas de vacaciones normalmente?	Voy con mi madre y mi abuela.
¿Cuánto tiempo pasas allí?	Fui a Grecia.
¿Con quién vas?	Visité pueblos típicos.
¿Dónde te quedas?	Voy a Irlanda.
¿Adónde fuiste el verano pasado?	Voy por dos semanas.
¿Qué hiciste?	Me quedo en una caravana.

[6]

2 Write the infinitives of these holiday activities.

Example: **Visito un parque acuático – visitar.**

a) **Vamos al zoo.** ....

b) **Saco fotos de monumentos impresionantes.** ....

c) **Hago ciclismo con mis primos.** ....

d) **Me relajo en la playa.** ....

e) **Voy de compras en las tiendas pequeñas.** .... [5]

3 Write this present tense sentence in the preterite tense.

Voy a las montañas en el invierno, me quedo en un albergue juvenil y hago esquí.

....

.... [3]

4 Read these descriptions of holiday destinations and write the name of the country in Spanish.

a) **Hace tres años fui a Nueva York. Me encantó el ambiente y vi muchos monumentos impresionantes y fui de compras en Macy's.**

....

b) **Me encanta visitar los museos famosos y edificios increíbles, por ejemplo la Torre Eiffel, y probar platos típicos, por ejemplo el bistec con patatas fritas.**

....

c) Hay muchas islas pintorescas e hicimos vela alrededor de ellas. Mi lugar favorito se llama Santorini, la puesta del sol fue increíble. La cultura griega me fascina y aprendí mucho.

_____

d) Lo malo es que el vuelo es muy largo, pero cuando llegas todo es asombroso. Desde las selvas tropicales hasta las playas impresionantes. La naturaleza es muy bonita y se puede ver canguros y los osos koala.

_____ [4]

5 Look at the descriptions in question 4 and find these words / phrases. Do not use a dictionary!

a) atmosphere _____ b) impressive _____

c) buildings _____ d) favourite place _____

e) I learnt a lot. _____ f) jungles _____

g) nature _____ h) you can see _____ [8]

6 Translate the following into Spanish.

a) I would like a double room for three nights.

_____

b) Is breakfast included?

_____

c) How much is a room with a view?

_____

d) The wi-fi doesn't work.

_____

e) The shower is broken.

_____

f) At what time is dinner?

_____ [6]

Total Marks _____ / 32

The Wider World

Global Issues

1 Draw lines to match up the global issues in Spanish to the translations.

El paro	the homeless
El hambre	unemployment
La pobreza	fake news
La guerra	globalisation
La globalización	hunger
La gente sin techo	poverty
Las noticias falsas	war

[7]

2 For each sentence put in the infinitive verb that best fits.

usar   respetar   tomar   ayudar   comprar   reciclar

a) Debemos _____ botellas y papel en casa.

b) Creo que la gente debería _____ menos ropa.

c) Intento _____ interés en la política.

d) Es importante _____ a la gente.

e) Todo el mundo debe _____ más el transporte público.

f) ¡Es importante _____ a los profesores!

[6]

3 Translate these sentences into English.

a) En mi opinión el mayor problema es el racismo.

_____

_____

b) La extinción de los animales, tal como el oso blanco, me preocupa mucho.

_____

[2]

_____

4 What are the concerns of these four people and what are they doing to improve the situation?

a) Hay tanta gente sin techo en mi pueblo y me hace sentir muy triste. Mi familia y yo donamos dinero a 'Crisis' una caridad que ayuda a estas personas.

Problem: _____
Action: _____
_____
_____

b) El calentamiento global me preocupa mucho y por eso soy miembro de un grupo ecologista que apoya a proyectos medioambientales.

Problem: _____
Action: _____
_____
_____

c) Leo mucho sobre el trabajo infantil que ocurre en países como Pakistán e Indonesia. Nunca compro ropa de tiendas que usan niños para fabricar ropa.

Problem: _____
Action: _____
_____
_____

d) El racismo en el mundo de deporte me pone furiosa. Esta semana escribí un blog en la revista de mi colegio sobre este problema.

Problem: _____
Action: _____
_____
_____

[8]

Total Marks _____ / 23

Grammar

1 Fill in the gaps in the table to show the correct articles of these animals. Look at the first one to help you.

A (singular)	A (in the plural)	The (singular)	The (plural)
un oso	unos osos	a) _____ oso	los osos
un caballo	b) _____ caballos	c) _____ caballo	d) _____ caballos
una gorila	e) _____ gorilas	la gorila	f) _____ gorilas
una serpiente	g) _____ serpientes	h) _____ serpiente	i) _____ serpientes

[9]

2 Write these words in the plural form.

a) el chico _____

b) la mujer _____

c) la ciudad _____

d) el centro comercial _____

e) el abrigo _____

f) el deporte _____ [6]

3 Choose the correct article to match the nouns.

Vivo en *el / los / las* a) _____ afueras de Santander en *el / los / un* b) _____ norte de España. ¡Me encanta vivir aquí! Me gusta mucho *la / el / las* c) _____ centro del pueblo porque *los / las / unas* d) _____ tiendas son muy variadas e interesantes. La única cosa que no me gusta es *la / los / el* e) _____ tráfico *los / las / el* f) _____ fines de semana. En *la / un / el* g) _____ futuro quiero vivir cerca de *la / un / las* h) _____ playa. [8]

Adjectives

1 Circle all the adjectives.

ropa	partido de fútbol	emocionante
largo	también	abuela
rubio	concurrido	español
caballo	gris	antipático
serio	pero	gato	gracioso

[9]

2 Write the antonyms (opposites) of these adjectives.

a) **corto** ....

b) **liso** ....

c) **pesimista** ....

d) **gordo** ....

e) **barato** .... [5]

3 Fill in each gap using an adjective in Spanish with the correct ending.

Hola, soy Katja y tengo dos hermanas a) .... (young). **Vivo en una casa**

b) .... (small) **en el campo de Andalucía, una región muy**

c) .... (pretty) **en el sur de España. Mi habitación es**

d) .... (comfortable) **y bastante e)** .... (big). **Hay una**

alfombra f) .... (grey) **y las cortinas son g)** .... (pink).

En el futuro me gustaría vivir en una ciudad h) .... (lively). [8]

Total Marks .... / 22

Grammar

tener, ser and estar

1 Draw lines to match up the two halves so they make sense.

| Mi prima |
| Soy muy |
| Mis hermanas son |
| Tengo |
| Mi pueblo |
| Mi padre y yo somos |

| creativa |
| disciplinados |
| el pelo corto y rizado |
| es deportista |
| bonitas |
| es aislado |

[6]

2 Choose the correct verb – either **ser** or **estar** – and make sure it is in the correct person.

a) **Mi colegio** _____ **lejos de mi casa.**

b) **Los perros de mi tía** _____ **muy tiernos.**

c) **¿Qué hora** _____**?** _____ **las tres y media.**

d) **En este momento mi abuelo** _____ **muy preocupado por la crisis económica.**

e) **¿De dónde** _____ **tu novio?** _____ **de Bolivia.**

f) **La capital de Italia** _____ **Roma.** [8]

3 Translate these sentences into Spanish.

a) I am 14 years old, and my sister is 19 years old.

_____

b) I live in Bilbao which is in the north of Spain.

_____

c) Are you thirsty?

_____

d) We are tall and thin.

_____

e) Where is the history teacher?

_____

f) I am in a hurry in the morning.

_____ [6]

Total Marks _____ / 20

Regular -ar, -er and -ir Verbs

1 Draw lines to match up these infinitive verbs.

hablar	to wear / carry
comprar	to understand
llegar	to learn
viajar	to talk
llevar	to buy
comprender	to run
aprender	to write
correr	to travel
escribir	to arrive

[9]

2 Write the following verbs in the first person, second person (tú) and 'we' form.

a) llegar ....

b) aprender ....

c) escribir .... [9]

3 Write the correct English subject pronoun / person. Example: **El médico** – he.

a) **Los abuelos** ....

b) **Mi hermano y yo** ....

c) **El profesor de matemáticas** ....

d) **Mis amigas** ....

e) **La gente** .... [5]

4 Choose the correct form of the verb to complete each sentence.

a) **Mi colegio** .... **(terminar) a las cuatro.**

b) **Mis padres** .... **(preparar) la cena.**

c) **Mi tía** .... **(correr) todos los días.**

d) **¿Dónde** .... **(trabajar)? Trabajo en la clínica.**

e) **Mis primos y yo** .... **(nadar) los fines de semana.**

f) **La gente** .... **(viajar) al extranjero en el verano.** [6]

Total Marks .... **/ 29**

Grammar

Stem-changing Verbs

1 Fill in the gaps in the table.

Empezar – to start	Querer – to want / love	Jugar – to play	Poder – to be able
empiezo	c)	f)	puedo
a)	quieres	juegas	i)
empieza	d)	juega	j)
b)	queremos	g)	k)
empezáis	queréis	jugáis	podéis
empiezan	e)	h)	pueden

[11]

2 There is one mistake with the verb in each sentence. Correct each error.

a) **Mis padres volan a Nueva Zelanda.** _____

b) **Me gusta juego al ping pong.** _____

c) **¿Queres venir a la fiesta? Sí, me encantaría.** _____

d) **La chaqueta costa 50 euros.** _____

e) **En mi insti las clases empezan a las 9.** _____

f) **Juegamos al golf los domingos.** _____

[6]

3 Answer these questions in full sentences in Spanish.

a) **¿Qué deportes juegas?**

_____

b) **¿A qué hora empieza tu colegio?**

_____

c) **¿Cuál asignatura prefieres?**

_____

d) **¿Qué piensas de las reglas en tu colegio?**

_____

e) **¿Puedes salir de tu colegio durante la hora de comer?**

_____

f) **¿Qué pides de postre en el restaurante?**

_____

[6]

Total Marks _____ / 23

hacer, ir and the Immediate Future

1 Match up these sentences so that they make sense.

Hacemos vela con	si tengo sueño.
¿Qué haces después	hace?
No hago mis deberes	solo.
Mis primos no hacen	mi abuelo.
Me gusta hacer ciclismo	del insti?
¿Qué tiempo	equitación en el invierno.

[6]

2 Translate the following sentences into Spanish.

a) I go to the beach in the afternoon. _____

b) My friends go shopping at 2 pm. _____

c) Where are you going? _____

d) My brother and I are going to the theatre on Saturday.

_____ [4]

3 Imagine you are Gemma and write sentences to say what you are going to do on Saturday. The first one has been done for you.

A las nueve y media voy a preparar el desayuno y luego voy a escuchar las noticias.

9.30 am	Make the breakfast and then listen to the news
11 am	Clean the house, work in the garden, it will be difficult
2.30 pm	Chat to my friends online and download music, it will be exciting
7 pm	Watch a film and drink a glass of wine, it will be relaxing

_____
_____
_____
_____
_____
_____

[9]

Total Marks _____ / 19

Grammar

Negatives and Impersonal Verbs

1 Translate these negative sentences into English.

a) **Nunca veo los programas de telerrealidad porque no me interesan.**

_____

_____

b) **No hay nadie en la cocina.**

_____

c) **Ninguno de mis amigos habla francés.**

_____

d) **No hacemos nunca natación si hace mal tiempo.**

_____ **[4]**

2 Read about Ignacio's weekend activities then rewrite the whole paragraph in Spanish.
Use impersonal verbs.

Los fines de semana I like to go shopping **solo**. I'm not interested in **las tiendas de ropa, pero** I love to go to **las librerías donde puedo encontrar libros sobre la historia y el arte. Las telenovelas y las películas románticas** annoy me **y prefiero estar en mi cuarto leyendo, aunque a mi hermana** she likes to **pasar tiempo chateando con sus amigas en línea, eso** I don't like it at all.

_____

_____

_____

_____

_____

_____

_____ **[6]**

Total Marks _____ **/ 10**

Preterite Tense

1 Draw lines to match up these time phrases.

el año pasado	yesterday
hace dos meses	two days ago
ayer	last year
anteayer	last week
el fin de semana pasado	two months ago
el domingo pasado	the day before yesterday
hace dos días	last night
anoche	last Sunday
la semana pasada	last weekend

[9]

2 Unravel these sentences.

a) pescado domingo el con comí mi pasado familia

b) pasado fuimos la el año playa a

[2]

3 Look at the information in the table and write sentences about Zofia and Alex's activities. Write in the preterite and in the first person. Example: **Imani – El sábado pasado fui al polideportivo, y jugué al tenis. Me gustó porque fue competitivo.**

Name	When	Where	Activity	Opinion
Imani	last Saturday	sports centre	tennis	liked it, competitive
Zofia	last night	park	cycling	relaxing
Alex	three days ago	beach	meet up with friends	fun

Zofia:

Alex:

[8]

Total Marks _____ / 19

Grammar

1 Look at Xavier's future plans and fill in the gaps with the simple future verb indicated.

Soy Xavier y este año es mi último año del insti. Tengo muchos planes para el futuro.

Primero, en septiembre a) _____ **(ir) a la escuela de formación profesional**

donde b) _____ **(empezar) un curso para ser electricista. En noviembre**

c) _____ **(trabajar) en un negocio por tres días con dos días en la escuela.**

Creo que d) _____ **(ser) exigente pero e)** _____ **(aprender)**

mucho.   **[5]**

2 Match up these irregular future verbs with their translations.

haré		I will say	
tendré		I will put	
podré		I will do	
diré		I will know	
pondré		I will have	
sabré		I will be able	

[6]

3 Translate these sentences into Spanish.

a) I will go to Paris next year and I will visit my cousins.

_____

b) In three months I will study science at the university, it will be demanding.

_____

c) I will be able to travel to the USA in the future.

_____

d) Next week I will do a Spanish exam, it will be difficult.

_____

e) Tomorrow my brother will help my parents in the garden.

_____   **[5]**

Total Marks _____ **/ 16**

Pronouns and Reflexive Verbs

1 Draw lines to match up these phrases.

Los visito	I want to see them.
Las ayudo	I want to eat them.
Las compro	I can hear it.
Quiero verlos	I visit them. (I am visiting them.)
Puedo escucharlo	I buy them. (I am buying them.)
Las quiero comer	I help them. (I am helping them.)

[6]

2 Replace the noun with the appropriate object pronoun.

Example: **Visito a mis abuelos después del colegio – Los visito después del colegio.**

a) **Veo las películas.** ....

b) **Como los caramelos en el cine.** ....

c) **Mi madre visita a mi abuela los domingos.** ....

d) **Quiero comprar los zapatos rojos.** .... [4]

3 Draw lines to match up these reflexive verbs.

Me ducho	I wake up
Me levanto	I get up
Me despierto	I shave
Me llamo	I shower
Me acuesto	I get tired
Me afeito	I go to bed
Me duermo	I fall asleep
Me canso	I am called

[8]

4 Put the first three verbs in question 3 in the third person.

a) ....

b) ....

c) .... [3]

Total Marks .... / 21

Grammar

1 Look at these English sentences and indicate which tense they are by writing in either **P** for preterite, **I** for imperfect or **PR** for present.

a) I always go to the beach with my friends in August. ....

b) When I lived in Newcastle I travelled to school by train. ....

c) Last Saturday I ate pizza with my parents. ....

d) I remember my French teacher because she was very strict. ....

e) I watch films at the weekends. .... **[6]**

2 Select either the preterite or imperfect verbs. Write your answers in the spaces below.

Antes a) .... *fui / iba* **a un colegio mixto en un pueblo en Asturias y**

b) .... *me gustó / me gustaba* **mucho. Hace 6 meses, mi madre**

c) .... *se casó / casaba* **con mi padrastro Thomas y ahora vivimos en el sur**

de España y tengo un nuevo colegio. Ayer d) .... *tuve / tenía* **una clase de**

historia y e) .... *aprendimos / aprendíamos* **sobre la Guerra**

Civil en España, ¡fue fascinante! Anteriormente no f) .... *me*

interesó / me interesaba **la historia, ¡pero ahora me encanta!** **[6]**

3 Translate the following sentences into Spanish. Remember that adding in a time phrase will signal the tense you are using and gain extra marks in an exam.

a) I used to eat fast food but now I eat more fruit and vegetables.

....

b) I often arrived late at school last year but now I get up on time. [on time – **a tiempo**].

....

c) My gran used to cook very well.

....

d) We used to go to France every year but last year we went to Ireland.

....

[12]

Total Marks .... / 24

Conditional Tense and deber

1 Answer these questions in Spanish. Use any conditional verbs in your answer, not just the ones in the questions.

a) ¿Qué te gustaría hacer en el verano?

b) ¿Cómo sería tu casa ideal?

c) ¿Cómo sería tu profesor ideal?

[9]

2 Translate these sentences into English.

a) Debo entregar mis deberes a tiempo.

b) Debería ayudar a mis padres en casa.

c) Creo que debería pasar más tiempo con mis abuelos.

[3]

3 Write four things you should do to improve the environment. Use **se debe / debo / debería**.

[8]

Total Marks _____ / 20

Mixed Test-Style Questions

1 Where would these activities take place? Write the locations in Spanish.

a) Mi equipo favorito de fútbol ganó el campeonato, el ambiente fue animado.

....

b) Me quedé en una habitación doble por tres noches. ....

c) Tuve que hacer un examen muy difícil hoy. ....

d) Vi una película de terror, lo peor fue que había mucha gente ruidosa.

....

e) Fui ahí para estar solo y para estudiar, no está permitido hablar en voz alta.

....

f) Probé el vestido, pero fue demasiado grande y muy caro. ....

6 marks

2 Read the weather forecast and then choose a picture for each town.

El tiempo para hoy.

Hoy el tiempo es muy variable en España. Llueve en Madrid, pero hace sol en Málaga. Hace calor en Barcelona, unos treinta grados, sin embargo, hace frío en Santiago, unos diecisiete grados. Está nublado en Murcia, pero en Cádiz en la costa hace viento.

A) B) C) D)

a) Madrid .... b) Santiago ....

c) Málaga .... d) Cádiz ....

4 marks

3 Imagine you are each of the people below. Write who you are and describe yourself in Spanish.

a) Elena: tall, green eyes and blond hair.

....

....

b) Felipe: small, brown eyes and short hair.

....

....

8 marks

4 A class of 30 pupils were asked what their favourite and least favourite colours are. Read the results below and then answer the questions that follow in English.

¿Cuál es tu color favorito?

Catorce alumnos han dicho: el rojo

Ocho alumnos han dicho: el verde

Seis alumnos han dicho: el morado

Dos alumnos han dicho: el gris

¿De qué color te gusta menos?

Diez alumnos han dicho: el azul

Siete alumnos han dicho: el rosa

Cinco alumnos han dicho: el rojo

Tres alumnos han dicho: el marrón

a) What is the most popular colour?

b) How many pupils do not like brown?

c) How many pupils said they did not like pink?

d) How many pupils mentioned red?

e) What colour has been mentioned most?

f) What colour did two students like?

6 marks

5 Draw lines to show which sentences fit together.

Tengo sed	¡La película es de terror!
Tengo hambre	¡Gané 50 euros!
Tengo prisa	Quiero beber agua.
Tengo suerte	ir al cine.
Tengo ganas de	No tengo mucho tiempo.
Tengo miedo	Voy a desayunar.

6 marks

6 Circle the correct verb / time phrase to describe Claudia's last holiday activities.

Hace 10 minutos / el verano pasado / el año próximo fui a Mallorca con mis padres y mi prima Ángeles. Cuando *llegamos / llegueamos / llegimos* era muy tarde, pero *hace / hago / hizo* mucho calor. El hotel *es / era / son* muy bonito y estaba a cinco minutos de la playa. Durante el día *hicimos / hace / hacemos* muchas actividades por ejemplo *fuemos / fui / fuimos* a un parque acuático ¡Qué divertido! La última noche *cenamos / desayunamos / charlamos* en un restaurante precioso que se llama Zaranda. ¡*Me encanta / Me encantó / Me encanté*! Quiero volver a Mallorca en el *pasado / futuro / último*.

9 marks

Mixed Test-Style Questions

7 Read the review of the book *Manolito Gafotas* and answer the questions in English.

Manolito Gafotas es un libro para niños escrito por Elvira Lindo y dibujado por Emilio Urberuaga. Es la historia de un niño Manolo o Manolito, un chico que vive en un piso con sus padres, su hermano pequeño y su abuelo, en un barrio que se llama Carabanchel, en las afueras de Madrid. Manolito es un niño muy travieso y gracioso. Su mejor amigo se llama Orejones López. Orejones es estúpido, pero amable. Junto con su pandilla, Manolito es capaz de vivir los hechos cotidianos como unas grandes aventuras estupendas.

a) Who is the book written for? ....

b) Who is the story about? ....

c) Where does the main character live? ....

d) Who is Orejones López? ....

e) Give one positive opinion that describes the main character. ....

f) Give one negative opinion that describes the main character. ....

g) Who does Manolito have adventures with? ....

7 marks

8 Choose the correct sport to go with each definition.

el esquí	el fútbol	el rugby	el tenis	la natación

a) Es un deporte de invierno. ....

b) Hay quince jugadores en un equipo. ....

c) Hay once jugadores en un equipo. ....

d) Voy a la piscina para practicar este deporte. ....

e) Hay que tener una raqueta y una pelota para jugar este deporte. ....

5 marks

9 Translate the following phrases into Spanish.

a) I don't like art because the teacher is strict.

....

b) My favourite subject is music because it is easy.

....

c) I hate science, especially physics.

....

d) Lessons start at half-past nine.

....

4 marks

10 Read Manolo's description of his school in Santa Cruz, Tenerife, and answer the questions below with true or false. Write **T** for true or **F** for false.

En Tenerife, en los colegios privados los alumnos llevan uniforme. El uniforme de mi colegio es azul. Los chicas llevan una falda azul oscuro con una blusa azul claro. Lo chicos llevan unos pantalones azul oscuro con una camisa azul claro. No llevan corbata. Hay unos veinte estudiantes en mi clase. Las clases empiezan a las ocho de la mañana y en verano no hay clases por la tarde. Mis asignaturas son: el español, el inglés, las mates, las ciencias, la historia, la geografía y el comercio. Me gusta mi colegio porque los profes son interesantes y nosotros los alumnos trabajamos muy duro.

a) All the pupils in Manolo's school wear blue clothes. ....

b) There are about thirty pupils in his class. ....

c) There are lessons in the morning only in summer. ....

d) He doesn't like his school. ....

4 marks

11 Draw lines to match up the two halves of the sentences.

Me encantan los conciertos	**fue genial.**
Mi compositor favorito es	**en el futuro.**
Prefiero los grupos británicos por ejemplo	**de rock.**
Ayer fui a ver la música en vivo y	**el piano.**
Voy a tocar el violín	**Coldplay.**
A mi hermana le gusta tocar	**Beethoven.**

6 marks

12 Write at least three things in Spanish that you are going to do in the future in relation to your studies.

....

....

....

6 marks

Mixed Test-Style Questions

13 Read this text message from Melissa and then write the details in English.

> Hola Lucía, ¿Qué tal? Vamos a ir a la pista de patinaje este viernes a las cinco de la tarde, ¿te apetece venir? Es mi cumpleaños el día siguiente así que ¡te invito yo! Después podemos volver a mi casa para comer pastel.
>
> Avísame si puedes venir...
>
> Un abrazo

a) Melissa is going to the .... at 5 pm.

b) It is her birthday on ....

c) Lucía won't need to ....

d) They will go back to Melissa's house to ....

4 marks

14 Describe your school uniform, mentioning at least three items, with three descriptions.

Para ir al colegio, llevo...

....

....

....

6 marks

15 Fill in the gaps with **al / a la / a los / a las / en / a**.

a) **Voy** .... **playa en el verano.**

b) **El año pasado fui** .... **Grecia con mis padres.**

c) **Estoy** .... **el centro comercial.**

d) **Antes iba** .... **tiendas cada sábado.**

e) **¿Cuándo fuiste** .... **Estados Unidos?**

f) **Vamos a ir** .... **museo con mi clase de historia.**

6 marks

16 Fill in the gaps with the correct words from the box. An extra word has been added to make this question more challenging!

adultos	martes	inglés	encantan	años	mucho	México

Me gusta a) .... **ver la tele y cada b)** .... **y viernes veo mi telenovela favorita que tiene lugar en c)** .... **. Me d)** .... **los actores y hay mucho suspenso. Recomiendo este programa para e)** .... **y niños de 12 f)** .... **o más.**

6 marks

17 Read what Marisol says about her job and answer the questions in English.

> Soy abogada y trabajo a diario excepto el domingo. Para ser abogada hay que ser trabajadora y tiene que disfrutar trabajar sola o en equipo. Hay muchas ventajas de mi trabajo, por ejemplo, es muy variado y está bien pagado, pero también es difícil y puede ser estresante. Cuando era más joven me interesaba la justicia y ahora soy abogada y me encanta mi empleo.

a) When does Marisol work? _____

b) What traits must you have to be a good lawyer? _____

c) What are the advantages of Marisol's job? _____

d) What are the disadvantages of Marisol's job? _____

e) What was Marisol interested in when she was younger? _____   8 marks

18 Choose two types of television programme and write your opinion of them in Spanish with a justification. Try to vary your vocabulary.

a) _____

b) _____   4 marks

19 What do you do with your pocket money? Write at least two things in Spanish.

_____

_____   4 marks

20 Write a possible question for each of these answers.

a) ¿_____ ? **Mi casa está cerca de la estación de tren.**

b) ¿_____? **Lo siento, no puedo ir al cine**
   porque ¡tengo tantos deberes!

c) ¿_____ ? **No hice nada anoche, me quedé en casa.**

d) ¿_____ ? **Fui a París por tres días.**   4 marks

Mixed Test-Style Questions

21 Fill in the gaps in these sentences about television using the words provided.

pero   ver   veces   nunca   ya que   verdaderamente   emocionantes

a) Veo las telenovelas dos _____ a la semana.

b) Veo las comedias _____ de vez en cuando son _____ aburridas.

c) Me gusta _____ los dibujos animados.

d) Me encantan las películas _____ son muy _____ .

e) No veo _____ las noticias.

7 marks

22 Look at this sentence and try to improve it by adding in a connective, an opinion and an adverb of frequency.

Visito a mis tíos que viven en la costa.

_____

3 marks

23 Answer this question in Spanish. Include a justification.

¿Qué te gustaría llevar al colegio?

_____

3 marks

24 Circle the correct school subject from the choice of three in each sentence.

a) Me gusta *la educación física / la física / la geografía* porque soy fuerte en ciencias.

b) Mi asignatura preferida es *la música / el dibujo / el teatro* porque me encanta tocar el violín.

c) Me gusta mucho *el deporte / la informática / el inglés* porque me mola trabajar con el ordenador.

d) *La historia / El español / La tecnología* es difícil porque no recuerdo las fechas importantes.

4 marks

25 Put these present tense sentences into preterite tense. Remember to add in a past tense time phrase.

a) **Siempre hablo español en clase.**

_____

b) **Arreglo mi dormitorio el sábado.**

_____

c) **Hoy voy al parque con mis amigos, ¡me gusta mucho!**

_____

7 marks

26 María is talking about whether school uniform should be introduced in Spain. Decide if the statements that follow are true or false. Write **T** for true or **F** for false.

> Muchos de mis amigos no están a favor de introducir el uniforme escolar, pero a mi modo de ver el uniforme escolar es una buena idea, porque no se notan las diferencias entre los pobres y los ricos. Hay un chico en mi clase que viene al colegio a menudo con ropa de marca. El uniforme es también práctico porque no hay que decidir qué llevar. Sin embargo, no me gusta nada la idea de llevar una corbata. Además, en Inglaterra, las chicas tienen que llevar un pichi o una falda, pero yo prefiero llevar unos pantalones.

a) Many of María's friends are in favour of having a uniform. ....

b) María is in favour of school uniform. ....

c) There is a girl in her class who wears designer clothes at school. ....

d) María thinks that wearing a uniform makes it easier to decide what to wear. ....

e) María likes the idea of wearing a tie. ....

f) She prefers wearing a skirt or pinafore rather than trousers. ....

6 marks

27 Look at these badly translated sentences. Correct the one error in each Spanish sentence.

a) I went cycling yesterday, it was great!   **Fui al ciclismo ayer, ¡fue estupendo!**

....

b) There are many people in the centre today.   **Hay muy gente en el centro hoy.**

....

c) I love my history teacher, he's very funny!   **Me encanta mi historia profesor, es muy gracioso.**

....

d) The clothes are very fashionable.   **La ropa son muy de moda.**

....

e) When is your birthday?   **¿Cuánto es tu cumpleaños?**

....

5 marks

Mixed Test-Style Questions

28 There are seven errors in total in the two sentences below. Rewrite each sentence with corrections.

a) Ayer fui a mi amigas casa y vimos una película romántica que me gusta mucho
porque fue aburrida, después comimos una pizza de jamón y tomate, ¡fui deliciosa!

....

....

b) Mi encanta mi profesor de química por que es muy comprensivo y nunca grito.

....

....

7 marks

29 Read Sofia's account of a meal in a restaurant and answer the questions in English.

> Para mi cumpleaños fui a un restaurante tradicional cerca de mi casa. Se come
> muy bien allí. Yo pedí el pollo asado con patatas fritas y una ensalada mixta,
> sin embargo, el servicio fue lento. Tuvimos que esperar una hora para el postre.
> Cuando, al final mi postre llegó, estaba frío.

a) Why did Sofia go to the restaurant? ....

b) Where was the restaurant? ....

c) What did she order? ....

d) What does she say about the service? ....

e) What was wrong with the dessert? ....

5 marks

30 Señor Valentín has a very busy week. Look at his diary and fill in the activities listed below in Spanish. Write the entries similar to the examples.

lunes	viernes
martes 9.30 cita con el dentista	sábado
miércoles	domingo 11.00–12.00 Pasear al perro con Ramón
jueves	

El lunes tengo que visitar a mi tía al mediodía.

El miércoles tengo una clase de guitarra a las dos de la tarde, dura una hora y media.

El jueves y el sábado trabajo en el café desde las 10 hasta las 6 de la tarde y el martes a partir de la una hasta las siete de la tarde.

No tengo nada que hacer el viernes en todo el día.

El sábado a las 8 de la noche voy a cenar en un restaurante italiano con mi novia Sabrina.

El domingo voy a ver una película al mediodía después de pasear a mi perro con Ramón.

7 marks

31 Fill in the gaps in the sentences below choosing an appropriate word from the box.

| las manzanas | los guisantes | el pollo | el queso | chocolate | sopa |

a) No me gustan nada las legumbres, sobre todo ....

b) Me encanta la fruta, por ejemplo ....

c) Me gustan las dulces y muchas veces como ....

d) Cuando hace frío, prefiero tomar .... de pescado.

e) Me gusta mucho .... como manchego o cabrales.

5 marks

32 Fill in this table with the relevant verbs in the first person.

Infinitive	English	Preterite	Present	Immediate future
ayudar	to help	ayudé	a)	voy a ayudar
comer	b)	c)	como	d)
hacer	e)	f)	g)	voy a hacer
tener	to have	h)	tengo	i)
j)	to play	k)	l)	voy a jugar

12 marks

33 Look at these time phrases and place them in the correct column.

| ayer ahora antes en el futuro la semana pasada el próximo mes en dos días |
| anteriormente hoy anoche en este momento hace tres semanas |

Preterite	Imperfect	Present	Future

12 marks

Mixed Test-Style Questions

34 Read Manuel's description of the Mexican town Oaxaca and complete the English sentences.

Vivo en Oaxaca que está situado en un valle y está rodeado por montañas. Se puede ver casas de muchos colores, iglesias impresionantes y ruinas arqueológicas. Es muy famoso por el arte y hay muchas galerías ahí. Se puede encontrar muchos estudiantes por todas partes. Desafortunadamente hay demasiados coches en el centro y causan mucha contaminación. Me gustaría ver menos basura en las calles y deben construir más zonas peatonales. Dicho eso me encanta la vida aquí porque siempre hay mucho que hacer y la gente es muy amable.

a) Oaxaca is situated in a _____ .

b) You can see multi-coloured _____ and _____ churches.

c) There are too many _____ .

d) There is too much _____ in the streets.

e) He likes the life in Oaxaca because there is _____ and the people are _____ .

7 marks

35 Complete these sentences about languages and nationalities.

a) En Suiza hablan francés, _____ e italiano.

b) Hablan _____ en México.

c) San Francisco y Nueva York están en _____ .

d) Leeds es una ciudad universitaria en el norte de _____ .

e) Edimburgo es la capital de _____ .

f) Hablan _____ en Quebec y Montreal que están en Canadá.

6 marks

36 Use the words in the box below to fill in the gaps in this shopping dialogue.

| rojo | 36 | comprar | cuánto | descuento | largos | probadores |

A: Buenos días, ¿qué desea?

B: Necesito a) _____ un vestido para la boda de mi tía.

A: ¡Muy bien! Tenemos vestidos b) _____ y cortos.

B: Pues creo que el estilo corto está más de moda.

A: Sí, tenemos este modelo en azul marino, c) _____ y verde.

B: Me encanta el azul marino, ¿tiene la talla d) _____ ?

A: Sí, aquí tiene, los e) _____ **están enfrente.**

5 minutos más tarde...

A: Este estilo me queda muy bien, f) ¿_____ **es?**

B: Hoy hay un g) _____ **de 20% en todos los vestidos, asi que cuesta 35 euros.**

A: Perfecto, ¡me lo llevo!

7 marks

37 Write sentences to compare these items using **más que / menos que / tan... como**. Use the adjective indicated.

Example: las naranjas y los limones [sweeter]

Las naranjas son más dulces que los limones.

a) El ruso y el inglés [more complicated]

_____

b) Las botas y los zapatos [less expensive]

_____

c) Las espinacas y el brócoli [as healthy as]

_____

d) El profesor de geografía y la profesora de biología [less strict]

_____

e) Ignacio y Mercedes [as hardworking as]

_____

5 marks

38 Fill in the gaps with **muy / mucho / mucha / muchos**.

a) Hay _____ **que hacer en Madrid.**

b) ¡Tengo _____ **deberes!**

c) Había _____ **gente en el supermercado ayer.**

d) Mi profesor es _____ **comprensivo.**

e) ¡Hace _____ **frío hoy!**

5 marks

Mixed Test-Style Questions

39 Fill in the gaps with the correct verb **tener / ser / estar**. You will need to change the verb to match the person. The first one has been done for you.

a) **Mi abuelo** *tiene* **setenta y ocho años**

b) **Mi prima** _____ **muy ruidosa.**

c) **Me llamo Diego y** _____ **peruano.**

d) **Mi padre** _____ **en el jardín hoy.**

e) **Me encanta mi colegio porque** _____ **muchos amigos allí.**

f) **Las matemáticas** _____ **útiles.**

5 marks

40 Change these present tense verbs according to the person.

a) **Mi colegio** _____ **(terminar) a las 4 de la tarde.**

b) **Mis padres** _____ **(hablar) inglés y francés.**

c) **No me gusta mi uniforme,** _____ **(llevar) una chaqueta verde y una falda gris.**

d) **El deporte es importante para mí, juego al golf, hago natación y** _____ **(correr).**

e) **Mi hermana y yo** _____ **(ver) mucho la tele.**

f) **¿**_____ **(cantar) bien? Sí, tengo clases de canto, ¡me apasiona!**

6 marks

41 Look at these sentences about hotels and correct the one error in each of the Spanish translations.

a) I want a double room for three nights.

Quiero una habitación doble por trece noches.

_____

b) The shower doesn't work.

La luz no funciona.

_____

c) Is dinner included?

¿Está incluido el desayuno?

_____

d) The room with a view costs £75.

La habitación con vista cuesta 75 libros.

_____

e) The lift is broken.

El ascensor está rojo.

....

f) I want to speak with the manager.

Quiero hacer con el director.

....

☐ 6 marks

42 Draw lines to match the foods with the correct type of cuisine.

el curry	la comida americana
los espaguetis	la comida japonesa
el sushi	la comida española
las tapas	la comida italiana
una hamburguesa	la comida india
el arroz	la comida china
el pescado frito	la comida inglesa

☐ 7 marks

43 Choose a word from each box to make up five present tense sentences on holiday activities.
Don't forget to change the verbs and add in **porque** (because).

Siempre	Hacer ciclismo	Me gusta	emocionante
A menudo	Ir de compras	Me encanta	genial
Normalmente	Visitar monumentos	Me interesa	relajante
A veces	Hacer natación	Lo paso bien	increíble
Cada día	Relajarse en la playa		me siento feliz
	Ir de excursión		porque es sano
	Ir a museos		aprendo mucho

....

....

....

....

☐ 15 marks

....

Mixed Test-Style Questions

44 Write a text message to your friend inviting them out.

Include the following:

- greet them
- suggest going to the cinema on Saturday afternoon
- say there is a Disney™ film on
- suggest going for pizza after the film
- end the text appropriately.

5 marks

45 Draw lines to match the sentences to the correct time.

Son las ocho y cuarto.	00:00
Son las nueve.	17:30
Son las once menos cuarto.	8:15
Es medianoche.	12:00
Es mediodía.	10:45
Son las cinco y media.	9:00

6 marks

46 Translate these sentences into Spanish – note that they are two-verb phrases.

a) I have to do my homework. ....

b) I should go to school on foot. ....

c) You should not waste paper. ....

d) I want to see my friends! ....

e) I like to buy clothes. ....

f) My mum likes to watch soaps. ....

6 marks

47 Read the opinions about celebrations in Spain and answer the questions that follow.

Daniela: Vivo en Valencia. A mí me encanta la fiesta de San Juan en junio. Hay muchos fuegos artificiales* y bailamos y escuchamos música toda la noche en la playa. A mi modo de ver es genial. *fireworks

Enzo: Pues, prefiero la Nochevieja. El 31 de diciembre salgo con mis amigos y festejamos con otros en el centro de Madrid. Contamos las campanas a medianoche, cantamos y comemos las uvas de la suerte. Es muy emocionante festejar en las calles.

Marta: Mi fiesta preferida es el día de Reyes, el 6 de enero. Recibimos los regalos de los Reyes y comemos el Roscón de Reyes**. En el Roscón hay una figura*** y también una judía****. La persona que tiene la figura es muy especial, es el rey o la reina para el día. Sin embargo, la persona que recibe la judía, tiene que pagar por el roscón el año próximo.

Arturo: Me encanta el Carnaval. Disfruto disfrazarme y cantar y bailar en las calles. Me flipan las procesiones, sobre todo en Santa Cruz de Tenerife.

** a sweet bread cake in the shape of a crown covered in fruits that represent jewels
*** a little figurine hidden in the cake
**** a small bean hidden in the cake

a) Who likes New Year's Eve? ....

b) Who likes Carnaval? ....

c) When do Spanish children receive presents? ....

d) Who becomes a king or queen on that day? ....

e) On what day do they eat lucky grapes? ....

f) In what month is the festival of San Juan? ....

6 marks

48 Read about the actor Alberto De la Ponce's daily routine and answer the questions in English.

Soy un actor colombiano y aquí esta mi rutina. Me levanto muy temprano porque me gusta pasear a mis dos perros. Después, preparo un desayuno de fruta y yogur, el fin de semana desayuno huevos y tocino. En este momento tengo que ir al Gran Teatro para ensayar porque voy a actuar en una obra del teatro en el verano. Vuelvo a casa y empiezo a aprender mis líneas, es muy difícil, pero ¡tengo que hacerlo! Para relajarme, llamo a mi hermano que vive en los Estados Unidos o juego a videojuegos. Al final del día me siento muy cansado y me acuesto a las 10 de la noche, pero si hay una buena película me acuesto más tarde.

a) Why does Alberto get up so early? ....

b) When does he have bacon for breakfast? ....

c) What is happening in the summer? ....

d) What does he find difficult? ....

e) Who lives in the USA? ....

f) Why does he sometimes go to bed late? ....

6 marks

49 Read Alba's blog on the pros and cons of technology and then fill in the table below in English.

> La tecnología es muy importante en mi vida, pero hay aspectos positivos y negativos. Primero, creo que la ventaja más grande es poder estar en contacto con los amigos todo el tiempo, pero puede ser también una gran distracción de los estudios. En este momento hago cursos en casa y es bueno poder aprender, pero cansa los ojos y no puedes estar con tus amigos. Además, me gusta mucho estar al día de las noticias, lo malo es que hay demasiadas noticias falsas. Me encanta ver vídeos en YouTube™ por ejemplo de mis artistas favoritos, pero es verdad que hay muchos vídeos violentos. Finalmente, mi amiga fue víctima del ciberacoso el año pasado y eso fue horrible.

Advantages of technology	Disadvantages of technology

10 marks

50 Fill in the table with the missing stem-changing verbs.

Infinitive	English	First person (I)	Third person (he, she, it)	'We' form
querer	to want / love	quiero	a)	queremos
empezar	b)	c)	empieza	empezamos
d)	to play	e)	juega	f)
poder	g)	puedo	h)	podemos

8 marks

51 Paula is remembering Gabriela who she used to go to school with. Put the verbs in brackets into the imperfect tense, which is used to talk about people you no longer see.

Gabriela era mi mejor amiga en primaria. Me a) _____ (llevar) muy

bien con ella porque b) _____ (ser) una persona muy amable y

comprensiva. Recuerdo que siempre c) _____ (tener) una sonrisa muy

bonita. En clase Gabriela d) _____ (hablar) mucho y los profesores le

e) _____ (dar) muchos castigos. Los sábados su madre nos

f) _____ (llevar) a la piscina. **g)** _____ (nadar)

durante una hora y después h) _____ **(ir) a comer pizza.**

☐ 8 marks

52 Translate the following phrases into Spanish. Use question 51 to help you.

a) I got on well with her. _____

b) I remember she had a nice smile.

_____

c) In class she used to talk a lot. _____

d) We used to go and eat pizza. _____

☐ 4 marks

53 Match up the Spanish and English equivalents of these greetings.

¡Hola!	Hello! / Good morning!
¡Buenos días!	See you later!
¡Hasta la vista!	Happy birthday!
¡Adiós!	Goodnight!
¡Buenas tardes!	See you again!
¡Buenas noches!	Hi!
¡Feliz cumpleaños!	Goodbye!
¡Hasta luego!	Good afternoon! / Good evening!

☐ 8 marks

54 Match up these opinions.

Pienso que	I agree
Encuentro que	On the one hand
Estoy de acuerdo	I find that
Estoy en contra	I think that
Por un lado	I am against

☐ 5 marks

Mixed Test-Style Questions

55 For each day of the week say one thing you are going to do. Use the immediate future tense.
Do not repeat activities! Example: **Lunes – Voy a comer pollo y patatas.**

martes	
miércoles	
jueves	
viernes	
sábado	
domingo	

6 marks

56 Look at these dilemmas and give advice using **tienes que / debes / deberías** + infinitive.

Beata:

a)
> Siempre como comida rápida por ejemplo
> hamburguesas y patatas fritas y nunca hago
> ejercicio… me siento muy mal…

Roberto:

b)
> Paso mucho tiempo en línea y nunca hago
> mis deberes, y mis profesores me dan
> muchos castigos…

Safrón:

c)
> Soy víctima del ciberacoso. Hay personas
> en mi colegio que escriben cosas falsas y
> horribles sobre mí…

6 marks

57 For each type of weather, write an activity you might do, for example:

Cuando llueve me quedo en casa y escucho música.

When it rains I stay at home and listen to music.

a)

b)

c)

6 marks

58 Complete the Spanish missing from each sentence.

a) Debo usar la _____ solar energy.

b) Debo ir en _____ public transport.

c) Cultivo _____ fruit and vegetables **en mi jardín.**

d) I have to _____ **comprar menos ropa.**

e) En casa debemos _____ switch off the lights **cuando no las necesitemos.**

f) No debería _____ waste paper.

6 marks

59 Read the following passage in which Dolores writes about health issues. Answer the questions in English.

> Es importante hacer deporte. El deporte es muy relajante y es bueno para la salud. También te encuentras con nuevos amigos sobre todo cuando juegas un deporte de equipo. Juego al balonmano a menudo con mis amigos. Voy a la piscina dos veces a la semana. No fumo nunca porque causa cáncer y los cigarrillos huelen mal también. Para relajarme, me gusta leer una buena novela o tal vez escucho la música. No tengo la intención de beber muchas bebidas azucaradas porque son malas para los dientes.

a) Why does Dolores say sport is important? Give three reasons.

_____

b) Apart from handball, what other sport does she do?

_____

c) Why does she not smoke? Give two reasons.

....

d) What two things does she do to relax?

....

e) What is she not going to do in the future and why?

....

10 marks

60 Look at the infinitive verbs below and make them into logical questions using the vocabulary in the box. Then translate the questions into English. For example:

llevar: ¿llevas vaqueros los fines de semana?

Do you wear jeans at the weekend?

canciones favoritas   vaqueros los fines de semana   chocolate caliente
a tus abuelos   un instrumento   en el patio   temprano al colegio
al ajedrez (chess)   un idioma (language)

a) gritar

....

b) jugar

....

c) beber

....

d) llegar

....

e) tocar

....

f) aprender

....

g) visitar

....

14 marks

Answers

Family (pages 148–149)

1. a) Felipe [1]
   b) Juan [1]
   c) Miguel [1]
   d) Alejandro [1]
   e) Marta [1]

2. a)-c) In any order: Mi cumpleaños es el seis de abril. [1]
   Mi cumpleaños es el diecisiete de noviembre. [1]
   Mi cumpleaños es el veinticuatro de septiembre. [1]

3. a) Marina [1]
   b) Sergio [1]
   c) Aurelia [1]

4. a) I have long, straight, brown hair. [3] I have blue eyes [1] and I am very tall. [2]
   b) I am quite short [2] and I have brown eyes. [1] I have short, black hair. [2]
   c) We are twins. [2] We have [1] ginger / red, curly, very long hair. [3]
   d) I have a small, white [2] cat. [1]

5. a) 6 is Miguel's birthday [1]
   b) 13 is Miguel's age [1]
   c) 40 is Marisa's age (Enriques's mum) [1]
   d) 43 is Pedro's age (Enrique's dad) [1]
   e) 14 is Lucia's age [1]

House and Home (pages 150–151)

1. a) Vivo en el sur de España. / I live in the south of Spain. [2]
   b) Mi casa se halla en el centro de la ciudad. / My house is in the city / town centre. [2]
   c) En nuestra casa hay nueve habitaciones. / In our house there are nine rooms. [2]
   d) No tenemos jardín. / We don't have a garden. [2]
   e) Nuestra casa tiene dos plantas y un ático. / Our house has two floors and an attic. [2]
   f) En la primera planta hay tres dormitorios. / On the first floor there are three bedrooms. [2]
   g) La habitación de mis padres está al lado de mi dormitorio. / My parent's bedroom is next to my bedroom. [2]
   h) Mi dormitorio es muy pequeño / bonito pero bonito / pequeño. / My bedroom is small / pretty but pretty / small. [2]
   i) En mi dormitorio hay muchas cosas. / In my bedroom there are lots of things. [2]

j) En mi dormitorio no tengo televisor. / In my bedroom I don't have a television. [2]

2. a) Mi casa es muy grande. [1]
   b) En mi dormitorio hay un ordenador. [1]
   c) Mis libros están en mi estantería. [2]
   d) El dormitorio de mis padres está al lado de mi dormitorio. [2]
   e) Mi ciudad está en el centro de España. [1]
   f) Mis primos viven en Murcia. [1]
   g) Mi abuela vive con nosotros. [1]
   h) Mi jardín es muy pequeño. [1]

3. ¿Dónde vives? —— Vivo en Alicante, cerca de la costa. [1]
   ¿Vives lejos de la costa? —— No, bastante cerca; está a unos diez minutos. [1]
   ¿Te gusta tu ciudad? —— Sí, porque mis amigos viven aquí también. [1]
   ¿Cómo es tu casa? —— Es bastante pequeña. [1]
   ¿Tienes jardín? —— Sí, y es muy grande. [1]
   ¿Ayudas a tus padres en casa? —— Sí, paso la aspiradora a menudo. [1]
   ¿Qué hay en tu dormitorio? —— Hay mi cama y mi armario. [1]
   ¿Tienes un ordenador en tu dormitorio? —— No, pero tenemos un portátil en el salón. [1]

Food and Drink (pages 152–153)

1. a) pescado €6 [1]
   b) zumo de manzana €2 [1]
   c) naranjas €3 [1]
   d) agua mineral €1 [1]
   e) bocadillo de jamón €4 [1]
   f) leche €1 [1]

2. a) Tortilla Española / Bocadillo de queso [1]
   b) Bocadillo de jamón / Bocadillo de queso [1]
   c) Tarta de limón [1]
   d) Sopa de tomate [1]
   e) Calamares [1]

3. Yo prefiero la cocina **italiana** porque me encanta la pasta y los **espaguetis**. Me mola la **pizza** de champiñones. De postre me chiflan los helados. Normalmente bebo un zumo de **naranja** porque no soporto las bebidas gaseosas, como la **limonada**. De vez en cuando tomo una bebida caliente como el café con **leche**, por ejemplo. [6]

4. a) P [1]
 b) P [1]
 c) N [1]
 d) P / N [1]
 e) P [1]
 f) P / N [1]
 g) N [1]

Sport and Health (pages 154–155)

1. El fin de semana me gusta ir a la piscina —— donde hago natación. [1]

El fin de semana me mola hacer equitación —— porque me chiflan los caballos. [1]

A menudo monto en bicicleta —— porque me flipa el ciclismo. [1]

Me encantan los deportes acuáticos —— como la vela. [1]

Me gusta ver partidos de fútbol, —— voy con frecuencia al estadio. [1]

Adoro el patinaje, —— pero me caigo a menudo. [1]

2. a) N [1]
 b) P / N [1]
 c) P / N [1]
 d) P [1]
 e) P / N [1]
 f) P [1]
 g) N [1]
 h) P [1]

3. a) G Water bottle [1]
 b) D Exercise [1]
 c) A Smoking [1]
 d) E Green tea [1]
 e) C Sleeping [1]
 f) B Cake [1]
 g) F Reading [1]

4. a) deportista [1]
 b) violento [1]
 c) natación [1]
 d) malo, cáncer [2]
 e) forma, verduras [2]

School and Education (pages 156–157)

1. a) G (Science) [1]
 b) C (English) [1]
 c) F (Sport / PE) [1]
 d) D (ICT / Computing) [1]
 e) A (Geography) [1]
 f) E (History) [1]

2. a) aburridas [1]
 b) deberes [1]
 c) aburrida [1]
 d) simpáticos [1]
 e) fuerte [1]
 f) libros [1]

3. a) T [1]
 b) T [1]
 c) T [1]
 d) F [1]
 e) T [1]
 f) F [1]

4. a) Arturo [1]
 b) Selina [1]
 c) Carmen [1]
 d) Carmen [1]
 e) Arturo [1]
 f) Carmen [1]
 g) Arturo [1]
 h) Selina [1]

Future Plans (pages 158–159)

1. después —— afterwards [1]
 el año próximo —— next year [1]
 luego —— then / next [1]
 en el futuro —— in the future [1]
 ante todo —— first of all [1]
 dentro de tres años —— in three years [1]

2. a) abogada [1]
 b) peluquera [1]
 c) directora [1]
 d) enfermera [1]
 e) dentista [1]

3. a) Voy a **dejar** el colegio. [1]
 b) Voy a **continuar** con mis estudios. [1]
 c) Voy a **ir** a la universidad. [1]
 d) Voy a **viajar** al extranjero. [1]
 e) Voy a **vivir** en una casa grande. [1]
 f) Voy a **tener** hijos. [1]

4. a) Necesito estar motivado. / I need to be motivated. [2]
 b) Tiene que cooperar con sus compañeros. / You need to cooperate with your colleagues. [2]
 c) Puedo comunicar mis ideas. / I can communicate my ideas. [2]

5. a) Translator [1]
 b) Because she can work alone or in a team. [1]
 c) Allows her to communicate with lots of different people. [1]

d) It is interesting and quite well paid. [1]

e) Work abroad as it would be satisfying
and exciting. [1]

Leisure (pages 160–161)

1. a) In the shopping centre, 11 am [1]

b) Outside the bowling alley, 8.30 pm [1]

c) Opposite the library, 9 am tomorrow [1]

2. ¿Te apetece ir a la —— bolera este viernes? [1]

¿Quieres comer después de —— ver la película? [1]

¿Tienes ganas de pasear —— a mi perro conmigo? [1]

¿Quieres venir al parque —— de atracciones
el sábado? [1]

Tengo una entrada para el concierto —— de rock
mañana, ¿quieres venir? [1]

3. Te apetece / te gustaría / quieres / tienes ganas de /
ir a la playa [1]

El domingo a las 2 [1]

Nos encontramos / te veo / quedamos fuera del café [1]

4. a) Voy a la piscina a la una. [1]

b) Voy a la biblioteca a las 10. [1]

c) Voy al parque a las 11.30. [1]

d) Voy al centro comercial a las doce / al mediodía. [1]

5. a) ir [1]

b) cuándo [1]

c) próximo [1]

d) puedo [1]

e) abuela [1]

TV and Technology (pages 162–163)

1. a) un dibujo animado [1]

b) un concurso [1]

c) una emisión / un programa de deportes [1]

d) un documental [1]

e) las noticias – el telediario [1]

f) una telenovela [1]

. b)-f) (no) Me gustan / me encantan / odio etc. +
programme + plural adjective [10]

. De vez en cuando —— sometimes [1]

Todos los días —— every day [1]

Nunca —— never [1]

Siempre —— always [1]

A menudo —— often [1]

Dos veces a la semana —— twice a week [1]

Raramente —— rarely [1]

. Siempre / a veces, etc. veo las emisiones de música
porque son entretenidas / divertidas, etc. [3]

5. a) vivo con mi madre [1]

b) me encanta ver las telenovelas [1]

c) tres veces a la semana [1]

d) miércoles [1]

e) demasiado tiempo [1]

f) estoy de acuerdo [1]

g) una película inglesa [1]

h) estupenda / genial etc. [1]

6. a) You can do **courses** at home. [1]

b) I can be in touch with my **uncles
and aunts**. [1]

c) I can **record** special moments. [1]

d) I can **look for** information. [1]

e) You can organise **going out / meeting up**. [1]

f) It **helps** me with my studies. [1]

Shopping and Money (pages 164–165)

1. a) Llevo unos pantalones azules de algodón. / I wear
blue, cotton trousers. [1]

b) Me gustan mucho mis zapatillas de deporte
blancas. / I really like my white trainers. [1]

c) Prefiero llevar vaqueros al colegio porque
son cómodos. / I prefer to wear jeans to
school because they are comfortable. [2]

2. a) Una camiseta verde y blanca. [1]

b) Una chaqueta negra de moda. [1]

3. d), b), a), f), e), c), h), g) [8]

4. a) child [1]

b) work in the garden [1]

c) fair [1]

d) a lot of [1]

e) saves [1]

f) clothes [1]

5. a) Recibo _____ libras / euros [1]

b) Any of: Hago la compra; Ayudo en casa; Cuido a
mi hermano menor; Trabajo en el jardín; Preparo
la comida; Lavo los platos; Arreglo mi dormitorio;
Pongo la mesa; Paseo al perro; No hago nada [1]

c) Gasto mi dinero en revistas / ropa / videojuegos,
etc. [1]

6. Reparto periódicos —— I deliver newspapers. [1]

Trabajo en una peluquería —— I work
in a hairdressers. [1]

Hago de canguro —— I do babysitting. [1]

Trabajo en una tienda —— I work in a shop. [1]

Ayudo a mis padres —— I help my parents. [1]

Where I Live (pages 166–167)

1. a) el mercado [1]
   b) el polideportivo [1]
   c) la biblioteca [1]
   d) la iglesia [1]
   e) el estadio [1]
   f) el museo [1]
   g) el jardín botánico / parque [1]
2. a) ¿Te gusta vivir en tu pueblo? [1]
   b) ¿Dónde vive tu abuela? [1]
   c) ¿Prefieres vivir en la ciudad o en el campo? [1]
   d) ¿Dónde está Brighton? [1]
   e) ¿Con quién vives? [1]
3. a) D, b) G, c) A, d) F, e) B, f) C, g) E [7]
4. a) East coast of Mexico [1]
   b) the USA [1]
   c) fine, golden sand [2]
   d) dive / scuba dive and see whales [2]
   e) beautiful views, nice people, pleasant climate [3]

Holidays (pages 168–169)

1. ¿Adónde vas de vacaciones normalmente? —— Voy
   a Irlanda. [1]
   ¿Cuánto tiempo pasas allí? —— Voy por dos
   semanas. [1]
   ¿Con quién vas? —— Voy con mi madre y mi abuela. [1]
   ¿Dónde te quedas? —— Me quedo en una caravana. [1]
   ¿Adónde fuiste el verano pasado? —— Fui a Grecia. [1]
   ¿Qué hiciste? —— Visité pueblos típicos. [1]
2. a) ir [1]
   b) sacar [1]
   c) hacer [1]
   d) relajarse (reflexive verb) [1]
   e) ir de compras (to go shopping) [1]
3. Fui a las montañas en el invierno / el invierno pasado,
   me quedé en un albergue juvenil e hice esquí. [1 mark
   for each correct verb in preterite.] [3]
4. a) los Estados Unidos [1]
   b) Francia [1]
   c) Grecia [1]
   d) Australia [1]
5. a) ambiente [1]
   b) impresionantes [1]
   c) edificios [1]
   d) lugar favorito [1]

e) aprendí mucho [1]
f) selvas [1]
g) naturaleza [1]
h) se puede ver [1]

6. a) Quiero / quisiera / me gustaría una habitación
   doble para tres noches. [1]
   b) ¿el desayuno está incluido? [word order flexible] [1]
   c) ¿Cuánto es (cuesta) una habitación con vista? [1]
   d) El wifi no funciona. [1]
   e) La ducha está rota / no funciona. [1]
   f) ¿A qué hora / cuándo es la cena? [1]

Global Issues (pages 170–171)

1. El paro —— unemployment [1]
   El hambre —— hunger [1]
   La pobreza —— poverty [1]
   La guerra —— war [1]
   La globalización —— globalisation [1]
   La gente sin techo —— the homeless [1]
   Las noticias falsas —— fake news [1]
2. a) reciclar [1]
   b) comprar [1]
   c) tomar [1]
   d) ayudar [1]
   e) usar [1]
   f) respetar [1]
3. a) In my opinion / I think that racism is the greatest /
      biggest problem. [1]
   b) Animal extinction, such as the white bear, worries
      me a lot. [1]
4. a) homeless people / donate money to charity
      [to help] [2]
   b) global warming / member of a green / eco group [2]
   c) child labour / never buy clothes from shops which
      use child labour [to make clothes] [2]
   d) racism in sport / wrote a blog [to highlight
      problem] [2]

Gender and Plurals (page 172)

1. a) el [1]
   b) unos [1]
   c) el [1]
   d) los [1]
   e) unas [1]

f) las **[1]**

g) unas **[1]**

h) la **[1]**

i) las **[1]**

2. a) los chicos **[1]**

b) las mujeres **[1]**

c) las ciudades **[1]**

d) los centros comerciales **[1]**

e) los abrigos **[1]**

f) los deportes **[1]**

3. a) las **[1]**

b) el **[1]**

c) el **[1]**

d) las **[1]**

e) el **[1]**

f) los **[1]**

g) el **[1]**

h) la **[1]**

Adjectives (page 173)

1. emocionante, largo, rubio, concurrido, español, gris, antipático, serio, gracioso **[9]**

2. a) largo **[1]**

b) rizado / ondulado **[1]**

c) optimista **[1]**

d) delgado **[1]**

e) caro **[1]**

3. a) jóvenes / menores **[1]**

b) pequeña **[1]**

c) bonita / preciosa [either answer] **[1]**

d) cómoda **[1]**

e) grande **[1]**

f) gris **[1]**

g) rosa **[1]**

h) animada **[8]**

tener, ser and estar (page 174)

1. Mi prima —— es deportista **[1]**

Soy muy —— creativa **[1]**

Mis hermanas son —— bonitas **[1]**

Tengo —— el pelo corto y rizado **[1]**

Mi pueblo —— es aislado **[1]**

Mi padre y yo somos —— disciplinados **[1]**

2. a) está **[1]**

b) son **[1]**

c) es / son **[2]**

d) está **[1]**

e) es / es **[2]**

f) es **[1]**

3. a) Tengo catorce años y mi hermana tiene diecinueve. [años] **[1]**

b) Vivo en Bilbao que está en el norte de España. **[1]**

c) ¿Tienes sed? **[1]**

d) Somos altos(as) y delgados(as). **[1]**

e) ¿Dónde está el profesor / la profesora de historia? **[1]**

f) Tengo prisa por la mañana. **[1]**

Regular -ar, -er and -ir Verbs (page 175)

1. hablar —— to talk **[1]**

comprar —— to buy **[1]**

llegar —— to arrive **[1]**

viajar —— to travel **[1]**

llevar —— to wear / carry **[1]**

comprender —— to understand **[1]**

aprender —— to learn **[1]**

correr —— to run **[1]**

escribir —— to write **[1]**

2. a) llego / llegas / llegamos **[3]**

b) aprendo / aprendes / aprendemos **[3]**

c) escribo / escribes / escribimos **[3]**

3. a) they **[1]**

b) we **[1]**

c) he **[1]**

d) they **[1]**

e) it [people is singular in Spanish] **[1]**

4. a) termina **[1]**

b) preparan **[1]**

c) corre **[1]**

d) trabajas **[1]**

e) nadamos **[1]**

f) viaja **[1]**

Stem-changing Verbs (page 176)

1. a) empiezas **[1]**

b) empezamos **[1]**

c) quiero **[1]**

d) quiere [1]

e) quieren [1]

f) juego [1]

g) jugamos [1]

h) juegan [1]

i) puedes [1]

j) puede [1]

k) podemos [1]

2. **a)** volan – vuelan [1]

b) juego – jugar [two-verb phrase] [1]

c) queres – quieres [1]

d) costa – cuesta [1]

e) empezan – empiezan [1]

f) juegamos – jugamos [1]

3. **a)** Juego al…. [1]

b) Mi colegio empieza a las… [1]

c) Prefiero…. [1]

d) Pienso que son… [1]

e) Sí / no puedo salir… [1]

f) Pido…. [1]

hacer, -ir and the Immediate Future (page 177)

1. Hacemos vela con —— mi abuelo. [1]

¿Qué haces después —— del insti? [1]

No hago mis deberes —— si tengo sueño. [1]

Mis primos no hacen —— equitación en el invierno. [1]

¿Qué tiempo —— hace? [1]

Me gusta hacer ciclismo —— solo. [1]

2. **a)** Voy a la playa por la tarde. [1]

b) Mis amigos van de compras a las 2. [1]

c) ¿Adónde vas? [1]

d) Mi hermano y yo vamos al teatro el sábado. [1]

3. A las once voy a limpiar la casa y trabajar en el jardín, será dfícil. [3]

A las dos y media voy a chatear con mis amigos / as en línea, y descargar música, será emocionante. [3]

A las siete voy a ver una película y beber un vaso de vino / una copa de vino, será relajante. [3]

Negatives and Impersonal Verbs (page 178)

1. **a)** I never watch television reality shows because they don't interest me. [1]

b) There is nobody / no one in the kitchen. [1]

c) None of my friends speak French. [1]

d) We never go swimming if it's bad weather. [1]

2. Los fines de semana **me gusta ir de compras** solo. **No me interesan** las tiendas de ropa, pero **me encanta ir a** las librerías donde puedo encontrar libros sobre la historia y el arte. Las telenovelas y las películas románticas **me molestan** y prefiero estar en mi cuarto leyendo, aunque a mi hermana **le gusta** pasar tiempo chateando con sus amigas en línea, eso **no me gusta nada**. [6]

Preterite Tense (page 179)

1. el año pasado —— last year [1]

hace dos meses —— two months ago [1]

ayer —— yesterday [1]

anteayer —— the day before yesterday [1]

el fin de semana pasado —— last weekend [1]

el domingo pasado —— last Sunday [1]

hace dos días —— two days ago [1]

anoche —— last night [1]

la semana pasada —— last week [1]

2. **a)** El domingo pasado comí pescado con mi familia. [1]

b) El año pasado fuimos a la playa. [1]

[Time can go at the start or the end of the sentence.]

3. **[1 mark for each of the following: correct time phrase, two activities and one opinion.]**

Zofía: Anoche fui al parque e hice ciclismo / monté en bici. Fue relajante. [4]

Alex: Hace tres días fui a la playa y me encontré con mis amigos. Fue divertido. [4]

[Time can go at the start or the end of the first sentence.]

Future Tense (page 180)

1. **a)** iré [1]

b) empezaré [1]

c) trabajaré [1]

d) será [1]

e) aprenderé [1]

2. haré —— I will do [1]

tendré —— I will have [1]

podré —— I will be able [1]

diré —— I will say [1]

pondré —— I will put [1]

sabré —— I will know [1]

3. **a)** Iré a París el año que viene y visitaré a mis primos **[1]**

b) En tres meses estudiaré las ciencias en la universidad, será exigente. **[1]**

c) Podré viajar a los Estados Unidos en el futuro. **[1]**

d) La semana próxima haré un examen de español, será difícil. **[1]**

e) Mañana mi hermano ayudará a mis padres en el jardín. **[1]**

[Time can go at the start or the end of the sentence.]

Pronouns and Reflexive Verbs (page 181)

1. Los visito —— I visit them. (I am visiting them.) **[1]**

Las ayudo —— I help them. (I am helping them.) **[1]**

Las compro —— I buy them. (I am buying them.) **[1]**

Quiero verlos —— I want to see them. **[1]**

Puedo escucharlo —— I can hear it. **[1]**

Las quiero comer —— I want to eat them. **[1]**

2. **a)** Las veo. **[1]**

b) Los como en el cine. **[1]**

c) Mi madre la visita los domingos. **[1]**

d) Quiero comprarlos or los quiero comprar. **[1]**

3. Me ducho —— I shower **[1]**

Me levanto —— I get up **[1]**

Me despierto —— I wake up **[1]**

Me llamo —— I am called **[1]**

Me acuesto —— I go to bed **[1]**

Me afeito —— I shave **[1]**

Me duermo —— I fall asleep **[1]**

Me canso —— I get tired **[1]**

4. **a)** se ducha **[1]**

b) se levanta **[1]**

c) se despierta (stem-changing verb) **[1]**

Imperfect Tense (page 182)

1. **a)** PR **[1]**

b) I **[1]**

c) P **[1]**

d) PR, I **[2]**

e) PR **[1]**

2. **a)** iba **[1]**

b) me gustaba **[1]**

c) se casó **[1]**

d) tuve **[1]**

e) aprendimos **[1]**

f) me interesaba **[1]**

3. **a)** Antes / anteriormente comía comida rápida pero ahora como más fruta y verduras. [legumbres] **[3]**

b) El año pasado a menudo llegaba tarde al cole / insti pero ahora me levanto a tiempo. [Even though last year is finished, it was a repeated action.] **[3]**

c) Antes / en el pasado / anteriormente mi abuela cocinaba muy bien. **[2]**

d) Antes íbamos a Francia cada año / todos los años pero el año pasado fuimos a Irlanda. **[4]**

[1 mark for correct time phrase and correctly formed verbs.]

Conditional Tense and deber (page 183)

1. **a)** Me gustaría ir / hacer / viajar, etc.... **[3]**

b) Mi casa ideal sería / tendría / estaría en... **[3]**

c) Mi profesor ideal sería / tendría, etc.... **[3]**

2. **a)** I should hand in / submit my homework on time. **[1]**

b) I should help my parents at home / in the house. **[1]**

c) I think I should spend more time with my grandparents. **[1]**

3. Debo / debería / se debe + any four, for example:

apagar las luces cuando no las necesites.

bajar la calefacción.

ir a pie al colegio.

ir en transporte público.

ahorrar agua.

cerrar el grifo cuando te lavas los dientes.

usar la energía solar.

cultivar vegetales y fruta en el jardín.

donar la ropa vieja. **[8]**

[1 mark for each verb and 1 mark for each appropriate noun.]

Mixed Test-Style Questions (pages 184–204)

1. **a)** el estadio **[1]**

b) el hotel **[1]**

c) el colegio / el instituto / la universidad **[1]**

d) el cine **[1]**

e) la biblioteca **[1]**

f) la tienda de ropa **[1]**

2. a) Madrid: B **[1]**
    b) Santiago: D **[1]**
    c) Málaga: A **[1]**
    d) Cádiz: C **[1]**
3. a) Me llamo Elena. **[1]** Soy alta. **[1]** Tengo los ojos verdes **[1]** y el pelo rubio. **[1]**
    b) Me llamo Felipe. **[1]** Soy bajo. **[1]** Tengo los ojos marrones **[1]** y el pelo corto. **[1]**
4. a) red **[1]**
    b) 3 **[1]**
    c) 7 **[1]**
    d) 19 **[1]**
    e) red **[1]**
    f) grey **[1]**
5. Tengo sed —— Quiero beber agua. **[1]**
    Tengo hambre —— Voy a desayunar. **[1]**
    Tengo prisa —— No tengo mucho tiempo. **[1]**
    Tengo suerte —— ¡Gané 50 euros! **[1]**
    Tengo ganas de —— ir al cine. **[1]**
    Tengo miedo —— ¡La película es de terror! **[1]**
6. El verano pasado; llegamos; hizo; era; hicimos; fuimos; cenamos; Me encantó; futuro (I want to return – future idea) **[9]**
7. a) children **[1]**
    b) Manolito (Gafotas) **[1]**
    c) Any from: In an apartment, in Carabanchel, on the outskirts of Madrid **[1]**
    d) Manolito's best friend **[1]**
    e) funny **[1]**
    f) naughty **[1]**
    g) his gang **[1]**
8. a) el esquí **[1]**
    b) el rugby **[1]**
    c) el fútbol **[1]**
    d) la natación **[1]**
    e) el tenis **[1]**
9. a) No me gusta el dibujo porque el profesor es estricto. **[1]**
    b) Mi asignatura favorita es la música porque es fácil. **[1]**
    c) Odio / Detesto las ciencias, sobre todo la física. **[1]**
    d) Las clases empiezan a las nueve y media. **[1]**
10. a) T **[1]**
    b) F **[1]**
    c) T **[1]**
    d) F **[1]**

11. Me encantan los conciertos —— de rock. **[1]**
    Mi compositor favorito es —— Beethoven. **[1]**
    Prefiero los grupos británicos por ejemplo —— Coldplay. **[1]**
    Ayer fui a ver la música en vivo y —— fue genial. **[1]**
    Voy a tocar el violín —— en el futuro. **[1]**
    A mi hermana le gusta tocar —— el piano. **[1]**
12. Voy a ir a la universidad. / Voy a continuar con mis estudios. / Voy a estudiar ciencias. Etc.
    [2 marks per sentence with a correct future intention.] **[6]**
13. a) ice rink **[1]**
    b) Saturday **[1]**
    c) pay / buy a ticket **[1]**
    d) eat cake **[1]**
14. Para ir al colegio, llevo una chaqueta **[1]** negra **[1]**, unos pantalones **[1]** grises **[1]** con una camisa **[1]** blanca. **[1]** etc. **[1 mark for the item and 1 mark for the colour.]**
15. a) a la **[1]**
    b) a **[1]**
    c) en **[1]**
    d) a las **[1]**
    e) a los **[1]**
    f) al **[1]**
16. a) mucho **[1]**
    b) martes **[1]**
    c) México **[1]**
    d) encantan **[1]**
    e) adultos **[1]**
    f) años **[1]**
17. a) Every day except Sunday **[1]**
    b) Hard-working and able to work alone or in a team **[2]**
    c) It's varied and well paid **[2]**
    d) It's difficult and stressful **[2]**
    e) justice **[1]**
18. Example: Me encantan los concursos porque son divertidos. (no) Me gustan / me encantan / odio, etc., las / los + programme, etc., porque son + adjective in plural. **[1 mark for each correct opinion and 1 mark for each correctly formed adjective.]** **[4]**
19. Compro revistas; Voy al cine, etc. **[Up to 2 marks per answer depending on length.]** **[4]**

20. a) ¿Dónde está tu casa? [1]

b) ¿Quieres / te apetece / tienes ganas de / te gustaría ir al cine? [1]

c) ¿Qué hiciste anoche? [1]

d) ¿Adónde fuiste de vacaciones? [1]

21. a) veces [1]

b) pero, verdaderamente [2]

c) ver [1]

d) ya que, emocionantes [2]

e) nunca [1]

22. Siempre / a menudo / a veces etc., visito a mis tíos que viven en la costa, me gusta, etc., porque es + adjective. [3]

23. Me gustaría llevar + item of clothing porque sería + adjective. [3]

24. a) la física [1]

b) la música [1]

c) la informática [1]

d) La historia [1]

25. a) Ayer / hace dos días / el sábado pasado, etc., hablé español en clase. [2]

b) El sábado pasado arreglé mi dormitorio. [2]

c) Hoy / ayer / el sábado pasado, etc., fui al parque con mis amigos, ¡me gustó mucho! [3]

26. a) F [1]

b) T [1]

c) F [1]

d) T [1]

e) F [1]

f) F [1]

27. a) hice ciclismo [you can't say 'I went cycling' in Spanish] [1]

b) Hay mucha gente [muy is 'very'] [1]

c) mi profesor de historia [you have to say 'the teacher of history'] [1]

d) La ropa es [clothes is singular in Spanish] [1]

e) ¿Cúando? [¿Cúanto? is 'how much?'] [1]

28. a) Ayer fui **a la casa de mi amiga** y vimos una película romántica, **me gustó** mucho porque fue **interesante** [or another positive word], después comimos una pizza de jamón y tomate, ¡**fue** deliciosa! [4]

b) **Me** encanta mi profesor de **química porque** es muy comprensivo y nunca **grita**. [3]

29 a) It was her birthday. [1]

b) Near her house [1]

c) (roast) chicken, chips and a mixed salad [1]

d) It was slow. [1]

e) It was cold. [1]

30. lunes – 12.00 visitar a mi tía [1]

martes – trabajar 1.00–7.00

miércoles – 2.00–3.30 clase de guitarra [1]

jueves – 10.00–6.00 trabajar en el café [1]

viernes – libre [1]

sábado – 10.00–6.00 trabajar en el café; 8.00 cenar con Sabrina [2]

domingo – 12.00 / mediodía ver película con Ramón [1]

31. a) los guisantes [1]

b) las manzanas [1]

c) chocolate [1]

d) sopa [1]

e) el queso [1]

32. a) ayudo [1]

b) to eat [1]

c) comí [1]

d) voy a comer [1]

e) to do / make [1]

f) hice [1]

g) hago [1]

h) tuve [1]

i) voy a tener [1]

j) jugar [1]

k) jugué [1]

l) juego [1]

33. Preterite: la semana pasada, anoche, hace tres semanas, ayer [4]

Imperfect: antes, anteriormente [2]

Present: hoy, en este momento, ahora [3]

Future: en el futuro, en dos días, el próximo mes [3]

[hoy could also be preterite if the time you were referring to was finished]

34. a) valley [1]

b) houses, impressive [2]

c) cars [1]

d) rubbish / litter [1]

e) lots to do, nice / friendly [2]

35. a) alemán [1]

b) español [1]

c) los Estados Unidos [1]

d) Inglaterra [1]

e) Escocia [1]

f) francés [1]

36. a) comprar [1]

b) largos [1]

c) rojo [1]

d) 36 [1]

e) probadores [1]

f) cuánto [1]

g) descuento [1]

37. a) El ruso es más complicado que el inglés. [1]

b) Las botas son menos caras que los zapatos. [1]

c) Las espinacas son tan sanas como el brócoli. [1]

d) El profesor de geografía es menos estricto que la profesora de biología. [1]

e) Ignacio es tan trabajador como Mercedes. [1]

38. a) mucho [1]

b) muchos [1]

c) mucha [people is singular in Spanish] [1]

d) muy [1]

e) mucho [1]

39. b) es [1]

c) soy [1]

d) está [1]

e) tengo [1]

f) son [1]

40. a) termina [1]

b) hablan [1]

c) llevo [1]

d) corro [1]

e) vemos [1]

f) Cantas [1]

41. a) trece — tres [1]

b) luz — ducha [1]

c) el desayuno — cena [1]

d) libros — libras [1]

e) rojo — roto [1]

f) hacer — hablar [1]

42. el curry —— la comida india [1]

los espaguetis —— la comida italiana [1]

el sushi —— la comida japonesa [1]

las tapas —— la comida española [1]

una hamburguesa —— la comida americana [1]

el arroz —— la comida china [1]

el pescado frito —— la comida inglesa [1]

43. [1 mark given in each sentence for correct time phrase, activity and opinion.]

Examples: Siempre voy de compras, me encanta porque me siento feliz.

Cada día voy a museos, me interesa porque aprendo mucho. [15]

44. ¡Hola! [1]

¿Te apetece / quieres / te gustaría ir al cine el sábado por la tarde? [1]

Hay / ponen una película de Disney [1]

Podemos comer pizza / ir a comer pizza después [1]

Un abrazo / adiós / hasta luego etc. [1]

45. Son las ocho y cuarto. —— 8:15 [1]

Son las nueve. —— 9:00 [1]

Son las once menos cuarto. —— 10:45 [1]

Es medianoche. —— 00:00 [1]

Es mediodía. —— 12:00 [1]

Son las cinco y media. —— 17:30 [1]

46. a) Tengo que hacer mis deberes. [1]

b) Debería ir al cole / insti a pie / caminar / andar al colegio. [1]

c) No deberías / no se debería / no se debe malgastar papel. [1]

d) Quiero ver a mis amigos. [1]

e) Me gusta comprar ropa. [1]

f) A mi madre le gusta ver las telenovelas. [1]

47. a) Enzo [1]

b) Arturo [1]

c) 6 January [1]

d) Whoever finds the figurine [1]

e) New Year's Eve 31 December [1]

f) June [1]

48. a) to walk his dogs [1]

b) at the weekend [1]

c) he is acting / performing in a play [1]

d) learning lines [1]

e) his brother [1]

f) watches a film [1]

49. Advantages: to be in contact with friends all the time; do online courses / learning; good for learning; watching news; watching videos on YouTube™. [5]

Disadvantages: distraction from your studies; tires your eyes; fake news; violent videos; risk of cyber bullying. [5]

50. a) quiere [1]

b) to start [1]

c) empiezo [1]

d) jugar [1]

e) juego [1]

f) jugamos [1]

g) to be able [1]

h) puede [1]

51. a) llevaba [1]

b) era [1]

c) tenía [1]

d) hablaba [1]

e) daban [1]

f) llevaba (she took us – third person) [1]

g) nadábamos [1]

h) íbamos [1]

52. a) Me llevaba muy bien con ella. [1]

b) Me recuerdo que tenía una sonrisa bonita. [1]

c) En clase hablaba mucho. [1]

d) Íbamos a comer pizza. [1]

53. ¡Hola! —— Hi! [1]

¡Buenos días! —— Hello! / Good morning! [1]

¡Hasta la vista! —— See you again [1]

¡Adiós! —— Goodbye! [1]

¡Buenas tardes! —— Good afternoon! /
Good evening! [1]

¡Buenas noches! —— Goodnight! [1]

¡Feliz cumpleaños! —— Happy birthday! [1]

¡Hasta luego! —— See you later! [1]

54. Pienso que —— I think that [1]

Encuentro que —— I find that [1]

Estoy de acuerdo —— I agree [1]

Estoy en contra —— I am against [1]

Por un lado —— On the one hand [1]

55. [Make sure all the second verbs are in the infinitive
and that there is no repetition of ideas.] [6]

56. a) Tienes que / debes / deberías comer fruta y verduras /
hacer deportes / ejercicio or similar. [2]

b) Tienes que / debes / deberías limitar tu
tiempo en línea / pasar menos tiempo en línea /
dejar tu móvil con tus padres. **[1 mark for
correct first verb, 1 mark for second
verb(s) in infinitve.]** [2]

c) Tienes que / debes / deberías hablar con tu
profesor(a), padres / un adulto/buscar ayuda.
**[1 mark for correct first verb, 1 mark for
second verb(s) in infinitve.]** [2]

57. a) Cuando hace sol, voy a la playa. [2]

b) Cuando nieva, juego en el jardín / parque /
afuera. [2]

c) Cuando hace frío, llevo mi abrigo y botas / ropa
calentita **[1 mark for weather phrase,
1 mark for activity.]** [2]

58. a) energía solar [1]

b) transporte público [1]

c) fruta y verduras / legumbres [1]

d) tengo que [1]

e) apagar las luces [1]

f) malgastar papel [1]

59. a) relaxing; good for your health; meet new
friends [3]

b) swimming [1]

c) causes cancer; smells bad [2]

d) read a book; listen to music [2]

e) drink sugary drinks, because they are bad for your
teeth [2]

60. a) ¿Gritas en el patio? / Do you shout in the
playground? [2]

b) ¿Juegas al ajedrez? / Do you play chess? [2]

c) ¿Bebes chocolate caliente? / Do you drink hot
chocolate? [2]

d) ¿Llegas temprano al colegio? / Do you get
to school early? [2]

e) ¿Tocas un instrumento? / Do you play
an instrument? [2]

f) ¿Aprendes un idioma? / Do you learn a
language? [2]

g) ¿Visitas a tus abuelos? / Do you visit your
grandparents? [2]

Acknowledgements

The author and publisher are grateful to the copyright holders for permission to use quoted materials and images. Every effort has been made to trace copyright holders and obtain their permission for the use of copyright material. The author and publisher will gladly receive information enabling them to rectify any error or omission in subsequent editions. All facts are correct at time of going to press.

Published by Collins
An imprint of HarperCollins*Publishers* Ltd
1 London Bridge Street
London SE1 9GF

HarperCollins*Publishers*
Macken House, 39/40 Mayor Street Upper,
Dublin 1, D01 C9W8, Ireland

© HarperCollins*Publishers* Limited 2021

ISBN 978-0-00-847052-4

First published 2021

10 9 8 7 6 5 4 3 2

British Library Cataloguing in Publication Data.

A CIP record of this book is available from the British Library.

Authors: Helen Farrar and Sherrie A Spinks
Publishers: Katie Sergeant and Clare Souza
Project Manager: Chantal Addy
Editor: Jill Laidlaw
Cover Design: Kevin Robbins and Sarah Duxbury
Inside Concept Design: Sarah Duxbury and Paul Oates
Typesetting Services: Jouve India Private Limited
Production: Karen Nulty
Index: Simon Yapp
Printed in the United Kingdom

This book contains FSC™ certified paper and other controlled sources to ensure responsible forest management.

For more information visit: www.harpercollins.co.uk/green